Once again, Falender and Shafranske have written a book that displays their strong commitment to enhancing the profession's understanding of the practice of supervision. It is a gift to faculty who teach a course in supervision and a gift to students who seek to become competent supervisors. It is concise but filled with wisdom. It is transtheoretical and provides pragmatic ideas to enhance one's supervision competency.

—**Emil Rodolfa, PhD,** Professor of Psychology, California School of Professional Psychology at Alliant International University, Sacramento

Are you looking for that first book to launch your practice as a clinical supervisor? This is the one! Filled with transcripts and anecdotes and solidly grounded in the evidence base, *Supervision Essentials for the Practice of Competency-Based Supervision* is just that: *essential.* Taking a metatheoretical and competency-based approach, this is a concise, eminently readable, and comprehensive guide for instructors and graduate students alike.

—**Steve McCutcheon, PhD,** Director of Psychology Training at VA Puget Sound, Seattle, WA

Falender and Shafranske start with the best practices—outlining what is the ideal supervisory relationship and how to develop a supervision contract with students—then acknowledge the reality of issues that arise in supervision, including when students have trouble with supervision. I have already consulted the chapters that help administrators understand the importance of supervision in a mental health training program. I recommend this book most highly.

—**Nadya A. Fouad, PhD, ABPP,** University Distinguished Professor and Chair, Educational Psychology, University of Wisconsin–Milwaukee

Falender and Shafranske are the leading contributors to the supervision literature. In this book, they offer supervisors and supervisees a practical, focused approach to developing the knowledge, skills, and attitudes necessary to become a competent supervisor and a competent provider of the highest quality clinical services and patient care.

—**Ronald H. Rozensky, PhD, ABPP,** Professor Emeritus, Department of Clinical and Health Psychology, University of Florida, Gainesville

Supervision Essentials for

the Practice of Competency-Based Supervision

Clinical Supervision Essentials Series

CLINICAL SUPERVISION ESSENTIALS

HANNA LEVENSON *and* ARPANA G. INMAN, Series Editors

Supervision Essentials for

the Practice of Competency– Based Supervision

Carol A. Falender
and Edward P. Shafranske

American Psychological Association • Washington, DC

Published by
American Psychological Association
750 First Street, NE
Washington, DC 20002
www.apa.org

To order
APA Order Department
P.O. Box 92984
Washington, DC 20090-2984
Tel: (800) 374-2721; Direct: (202) 336-5510
Fax: (202) 336-5502; TDD/TTY: (202) 336-6123
Online: www.apa.org/pubs/books
E-mail: order@apa.org

In the U.K., Europe, Africa, and the Middle East, copies may be ordered from
American Psychological Association
3 Henrietta Street
Covent Garden, London
WC2E 8LU England

Typeset in Minion by Circle Graphics, Inc., Columbia, MD

Printer: Bookmasters, Ashland, Ohio
Cover Designer: Mercury Publishing Services, Inc., Rockville, MD

The opinions and statements published are the responsibility of the authors, and such opinions and statements do not necessarily represent the policies of the American Psychological Association.

Library of Congress Cataloging-in-Publication Data

Names: Falender, Carol A., author. | Shafranske, Edward P., author.
Title: Supervision essentials for the practice of competency-based supervision / Carol A. Falender and Edward P. Shafranske.
Description: Washington, DC : American Psychological Association, [2017] | Series: Clinical supervision essentials series | Includes bibliographical references and index.
Identifiers: LCCN 2016012630 | ISBN 9781433823121 | ISBN 1433823128
Subjects: LCSH: Clinical psychologists—Supervision of.
Classification: LCC RC467.7 .F356 2017 | DDC 616.001/9—dc23
LC record available at https://lccn.loc.gov/2016012630

British Library Cataloguing-in-Publication Data
A CIP record is available from the British Library.

Printed in the United States of America
First Edition

http://dx.doi.org/10.1037/15962-000

14 13 12 11 10 9 8 7 6 5 4 3

Contents

Foreword to the Clinical Supervision Essentials Series

We are both clinical supervisors. We teach courses on supervision of students who are in training to become therapists. We give workshops on supervision and consult with supervisors about their supervision practices. We write and do research on the topic. To say we eat and breathe supervision might be a little exaggerated, but only slightly. We are fully invested in the field and in helping supervisors provide the most informed and helpful guidance to those learning the profession. We also are committed to helping supervisees/ consultees/trainees become better collaborators in the supervisory endeavor by understanding their responsibilities in the supervisory process.

What is supervision? Supervision is critical to the practice of therapy. As stated by Edward Watkins[1] in the *Handbook of Psychotherapy Supervision*, "Without the enterprise of psychotherapy supervision,... the practice of psychotherapy would become highly suspect and would or should cease to exist" (p. 603).

Supervision has been defined as

> an intervention provided by a more senior member of a profession to a more junior colleague or colleagues who typically (but not always) are members of that same profession. This relationship
>
> ■ is evaluative and hierarchical,
> ■ extends over time, and

---

[1] Watkins, C. E., Jr. (Ed.). (1997). *Handbook of psychotherapy supervision*. New York, NY: Wiley.

■ has the simultaneous purposes of enhancing the professional functioning of the more junior person(s); monitoring the quality of professional services offered to the clients that she, he, or they see; and
serving as a gatekeeper for the particular profession the supervisee
seeks to enter. (p. 9)[2]

It is now widely acknowledged in the literature that supervision is a
"distinct activity" in its own right.[3] One cannot assume that being an excellent therapist generalizes to being an outstanding supervisor. Nor can one
imagine that good supervisors can just be "instructed" in how to supervise
through purely academic, didactic means.

So how does one become a good supervisor?

Supervision is now recognized as a core competency domain for psychologists[4,5] and other mental health professionals. Guidelines have been
created to facilitate the provision of competent supervision across professional groups and internationally (e.g., American Psychological Association,[6] American Association of Marriage and Family Therapy,[7] British
Psychological Society,[8,9] Canadian Psychological Association[10]).

---

[2] Bernard, J. M., & Goodyear, R. K. (2014). *Fundamentals of clinical supervision* (5th ed.). Boston, MA: Pearson.

[3] Bernard, J. M., & Goodyear, R. K. (2014). *Fundamentals of clinical supervision* (5th ed.). Boston, MA: Pearson.

[4] Fouad, N., Grus, C. L., Hatcher, R. L., Kaslow, N. J., Hutchings, P. S., Madson, M. B., . . . Crossman, R. E. (2009). Competency benchmarks: A model for understanding and measuring competence in professional psychology across training levels. *Training and Education in Professional Psychology, 3* (4 Suppl.), S5–S26. http://dx.doi.org/10.1037/a0015832

[5] Kaslow, N. J., Rubin, N. J., Bebeau, M. J., Leigh, I. W., Lichtenberg, J. W., Nelson, P. D., . . . Smith, I. L. (2007). Guiding principles and recommendations for the assessment of competence. *Professional Psychology: Research and Practice, 38,* 441–51. http://dx.doi.org/10.1037/0735-7028.38.5.441

[6] American Psychological Association. (2014). *Guidelines for clinical supervision in health service psychology.* Retrieved from http://www.apa.org/about/policy/guidelines-supervision.pdf

[7] American Association of Marriage and Family Therapy. (2007). *AAMFT approved supervisor designa-tion standards and responsibilities handbook.* Retrieved from http://www.aamft.org/imis15/Documents/Approved_Supervisor_handbook.pdf

[8] British Psychological Society. (2003). *Policy guidelines on supervision in the practice of clinical psychology.* Retrieved from http://www.conatus.co.uk/assets/uploaded/downloads/policy_and_guidelines_on_supervision.pdf

[9] British Psychological Society. (2010). *Professional supervision: Guidelines for practice for educational psychol-ogists.* Retrieved from http://www.ucl.ac.uk/educational-psychology/resources/DECP%20Supervision%20report%20Nov%202010.pdf

[10] Canadian Psychological Association. (2009). *Ethical guidelines for supervision in psychology: Teach-ing, research, practice and administration.* Retrieved from http://www.cpa.ca/docs/File/Ethics/EthicalGuidelinesSupervisionPsychologyMar2012.pdf

The *Guidelines for Clinical Supervision in Health Service Psychology*[11] are built on several assumptions, specifically that supervision

- requires formal education and training;
- prioritizes the care of the client/patient and the protection of the public;
- focuses on the acquisition of competence by and the professional development of the supervisee;
- requires supervisor competence in the foundational and functional competency domains being supervised;
- is anchored in the current evidence base related to supervision and the competencies being supervised;
- occurs within a respectful and collaborative supervisory relationship that includes facilitative and evaluative components and is established, maintained, and repaired as necessary;
- entails responsibilities on the part of the supervisor and supervisee;
- intentionally infuses and integrates the dimensions of diversity in all aspects of professional practice;
- is influenced by both professional and personal factors, including values, attitudes, beliefs, and interpersonal biases;
- is conducted in adherence to ethical and legal standards;
- uses a developmental and strength-based approach;
- requires reflective practice and self-assessment by the supervisor and supervisee;
- incorporates bidirectional feedback between the supervisor and supervisee;
- includes evaluation of the acquisition of expected competencies by the supervisee;
- serves a gatekeeping function for the profession; and
- is distinct from consultation, personal psychotherapy, and mentoring.

The importance of supervision can be attested to by the increase in state laws and regulations that certify supervisors and the required multiple supervisory practica and internships that graduate students in all professional

---

[11] American Psychological Association. (2014). *Guidelines for clinical supervision in health service psychology.* Retrieved from http://www.apa.org/about/policy/guidelines-supervision.pdf

programs must complete. Furthermore, research has confirmed[12] the high prevalence of supervisory responsibilities among practitioners—specifically that between 85% and 90% of all therapists eventually become clinical supervisors within the first 15 years of practice.

So now we see the critical importance of good supervision and its high prevalence. We also have guidelines for its competent practice and an impressive list of objectives. But is this enough to become a good supervisor? Not quite. One of the best ways to learn is from highly regarded supervisors—the experts in the field—those who have the procedural knowledge[13] to know what to do, when, and why.

Which leads us to our motivation for creating this series. As we looked around for materials that would help us supervise, teach, and research clinical supervision, we were struck by the lack of a coordinated effort to present the essential models of supervision in both a didactic and experiential form through the lens of expert supervisors. What seemed to be needed was a forum where the experts in the field—those with the knowledge *and* the practice—present the basics of their approaches in a readable, accessible, concise fashion and demonstrate what they do in a real supervisory session. The need, in essence, was for a showcase of best practices.

This series, then, is an attempt to do just that. We considered the major approaches to supervisory practice—those that are based on theoretical orientation and those that are metatheoretical. We surveyed psychologists, teachers, clinical supervisors, and researchers domestically and internationally working in the area of supervision. We asked them to identify specific models to include and who they would consider to be experts in this area. We also asked this community of colleagues to identify key issues that typically need to be addressed in supervision sessions. Through this consensus building, we came up with a dream team of 11 supervision experts who not only have developed a working model of supervision but also have been in the trenches as clinical supervisors for years.

---

[12] Rønnestad, M. H., Orlinsky, D. E., Parks, B. K., & Davis, J. D. (1997). Supervisors of psychotherapy: Mapping experience level and supervisory confidence. *European Psychologist, 2*, 191–201.

[13] Schön, D. A. (1987). *Educating the reflective practitioner: Toward a new design for teaching and learning in the professions.* San Francisco, CA: Jossey-Bass.

We asked each expert to write a concise book elucidating her or his approach to supervision. This included highlighting the essential dimensions/key principles, methods/techniques, and structure/process involved, the research evidence for the model, and how common supervisory issues are handled. Furthermore, we asked each author to elucidate the supervisory process by devoting a chapter describing a supervisory session in detail, including transcripts of real sessions, so that the readers could see how the model comes to life in the reality of the supervisory encounter.

In addition to these books, each expert filmed an actual supervisory session with a supervisee so that her or his approach could be demonstrated in practice. APA Books has produced these videos as a series and they are available as DVDs (http://www.apa.org/pubs/videos). Each of these books and videos can be used together or independently, as part of the series or alone, for the reader aspiring to learn how to supervise, for supervisors wishing to deepen their knowledge, for trainees wanting to be better supervisees, for teachers of courses on supervision, and for researchers investigating this pedagogical process.

ABOUT THIS BOOK

In this book, *Supervision Essentials for the Practice of Competency-Based Supervision*, Carol A. Falender and Edward P. Shafranske present a metatheoretical approach that highlights the knowledge, skills, attitudes, values, and ethics required to engage in effective and accountable supervision. Such foundational elements are key to helping supervisees demonstrate competence in their clinical work.

Falender and Shafranske view competence as an evolving process that is context driven rather than a finite point in one's development. In keeping with this, the approach requires supervisors to be intentional in their observations and assessments, anchoring their feedback in behavioral terms. Initiating the relationship with a supervisory contract, supervision consists of learning cycles that emphasize direct observation of a supervisee's clinical work. Through a focus on reflective practice, and the provision of ongoing evaluation and feedback, the supervisor helps plan clinical interventions. Each element in the learning cycle sequence captures the knowledge, skills and attitudes involved in the provision of clinical services. Above all, supervision is embedded in a supervisory alliance that underscores the interpersonal strengths of the supervisor and the power differentials in the relationship. Attention is given to personal and multicultural factors and self-care. Using various techniques, the supervisor models and helps supervisees develop metacompetence—the ability to know what one knows and does not know.

Competency-based supervision is a complex yet comprehensive transtheoretical model. In a systematic and a deliberate manner, Falender and Shafranske bring alive different concepts through thought provoking case examples, transcripts of live sessions, and reflective comments. In the following pages, the authors present a practical and hands-on approach to developing competency as a supervisor and a clinician.

We thank you for your interest and hope the books in this series enhance your work in a stimulating and relevant way.

Hanna Levenson and Arpana G. Inman

FOUNDATIONS OF COMPETENCY-BASED CLINICAL SUPERVISION

1

Groundwork and Rationale

A sea change has occurred in clinical training and supervision, reflecting a new era of accountability. As in other health care professions, such as medicine, it is no longer sufficient in clinical and counseling psychology to assume that competence is routinely attained through the accumulation of academic and training experiences. This emerging "culture of competence" (Roberts, Borden, Christiansen, & Lopez, 2005) requires the demonstration of specific competencies that are used in clinical practice (Falender & Shafranske, 2012b). *Competency-based clinical supervision* orients the supervisor and supervisee to the task of developing professional competence by providing structures and processes designed to achieve this training objective. This volume presents a practical guide to implementing the approach and is intended for both novice and experienced supervisors who are seeking to enhance the effectiveness of their supervision practice. We begin with a brief introduction to clinical supervision.

http://dx.doi.org/10.1037/15962-001
Supervision Essentials for the Practice of Competency-Based Supervision, by C. A. Falender and E. P. Shafranske

RESPONSIBILITIES AND FUNCTIONS OF CLINICAL SUPERVISION

Clinical supervision is the cornerstone of graduate education and clinical training in which a student of psychology gradually develops clinical competence and prepares to become a health service provider as a licensed psychologist (Falender & Shafranske, 2004). In addition to honing clinical skills, supervisees are assimilated into the profession, internalizing its principles, ethics, and values, establishing a foundation for lifelong practice. Although training is a major focus, the supervisor's first responsibility is always to the welfare of the client or patient.[1] The tasks of ensuring patient welfare and facilitating professional development, although distinct responsibilities, are inextricably interrelated. Given their multiple obligations to patients, supervisees, and the profession, supervisors must develop a clear understanding of clinical supervision and incorporate best practices to ensure competence and effectiveness.

DEFINING CLINICAL SUPERVISION

What precisely is clinical supervision? Definitions abound, reflecting differences in comprehensiveness and emphasis (Bernard & Goodyear, 2014; Falender & Shafranske, 2004; Milne, 2014), which may account for much of the variety of experiences supervisees have during their course of clinical training. We define *clinical supervision* as

> a distinct professional practice that requires balancing the inherent power differential within a collaborative relationship while utilizing both facilitative and evaluative components. It has the multiple goals of monitoring the quality of services provided to clients; protecting the public and gatekeeping for the profession; and enhancing the professional competence and professionalism of the supervisee,

---

[1]We are mindful that the use of the terms *patient* or *client* to refer to consumers of psychological services reflects theoretical, historical, and contextual background. In this volume, we use *client* and *patient* interchangeably, given the variety of clinical cultures in which supervision is offered and in which this volume is intended for use.

including developing skill in the use of science-informed assessment procedures, empirically-supported treatments and evidence-based practices. Clinical supervision is experiential, and involves observation, evaluation, feedback, facilitation of supervisee self-reflection and self-assessment, use of didactic and experiential learning approaches, and is conducted in a manner sensitive to individual differences and multicultural context and in which ethical standards, legal prescriptions, and professional practices are used to promote integrity and welfare of the client and communities. (based on Falender & Shafranske, 2004)

This definition is consistent with the *Guidelines for Clinical Supervision in Health Service Psychology*, recently adopted by the American Psychological Association (APA; 2014, 2015), which now serves as policy and defines and directs the practice of clinical supervision:

Supervision is a distinct professional practice employing a collaborative relationship that has both facilitative and evaluative components, that extends over time, which has the goals of enhancing the professional competence and science-informed practice of the supervisee, monitoring the quality of services provided, protecting the public, and providing a gatekeeping function for entry into the profession. (APA, 2014, p. 5)

Attention to the aims of supervision, as articulated in this definition, and implementation of the associated guidelines to achieve these objectives require a values-based commitment to the highest standards of the profession, in addition to specific knowledge, skills, and attitudes required to competently conduct supervision. Competency-based clinical supervision provides a comprehensive, systematic, and metatheoretical approach to implementing the *Guidelines* that can be applied to all clinical specialties and theoretical orientations. Given its explicit orientation to competency assessment and development, it is uniquely suited to achieve the heightened requirements of accountability within education and clinical training in health service psychology.

ADVANCING THE NEW ERA OF
COMPETENCY-BASED CLINICAL SUPERVISION

Most psychologists believe they are competent to supervise because they have been supervised and, thus, by indirect modeling, know how to supervise. This notion seems widely held, given that most supervisors describe their own personal experience as a supervisee as having the largest influence on their current supervision practice (Genuchi, Rings, Germek, & Cornish, 2015; Rings, Genuchi, Hall, Angelo, & Cornish, 2009). This presumption, that competence to perform supervision is sufficiently established without formal training ignores the complexity of the supervisory process and, further, may lead to the perpetuation of inadequate or poor practices, resulting in marginally effective or even substantially ineffective supervision. These concerns are quite real given the growing awareness that many supervisees have experienced inadequate, lousy (Magnuson, Wilcoxon, & Norem, 2000), harmful (Ellis et al., 2014), or failed supervision (Ladany, 2014). Conducting supervision solely on the basis of past experiences as a consumer of supervision (or efforts to do the opposite of the supervision received) does not furnish an adequate basis for practice. Now acknowledged as a distinct professional practice, clinical supervision requires competence in its performance—competence that is obtained not through osmosis but through specific education and training. As in other professional activities, competence in supervision practice involves evidence-based practice (APA Presidential Task Force on Evidence-Based Practice, 2006) that draws on sound theory, uses empirically supported procedures, considers supervisor and supervisee expertise, and is sensitive to culture and context.

It is ironic that a function so central to the development of clinical competence has been so neglected as a competence itself. It is equally surprising (if not disturbing) that clinical supervision, in contrast to other professional services (e.g., psychological assessment, psychotherapy), has not required specific graduate education and training for its performance. The Association of State and Provincial Psychology Boards (ASPPB) Task Force on Supervision (ASPPB, 2003) expressed similar concern at the lack of training and clarity for such, given the critical role of supervision in the protection of the public, and recently provided revised regulatory guidelines for training, practice, and conduct in supervision (ASPPB, 2015). Although this volume does not directly address regulatory issues, it does provide a framework for the conduct of clinical supervision that is in keeping with standards and guidelines.

What We Mean by Competence

A starting point to consider: What do we mean when we ascribe competence to a supervisor? Reflect for a moment on a supervisor you consider to be highly competent. What stands out? Each of us has notions about competence (and often can identify when it is lacking), but what criteria or standards should we use as psychologists and supervisors to orient professional development? *Competence* is generally understood to mean that one is qualified and capable of performing a specific professional function in an effective manner (Kaslow, 2004). This is a good starting point, but competence actually involves more than the performance of specific technical tasks. Rather, it includes many abilities, such as the translation of knowledge into practice, critical judgment, interpersonal skills, metacompetence, and ethical conduct, to name a few. A widely accepted definition, drawn from medicine, describes competence to be "the habitual and judicious use of communication, knowledge, technical skills, clinical reasoning, emotions, values, and reflection in daily practice for the benefit of the individual and the community being served" (Epstein & Hundert, 2002, p. 226). Epstein and Hundert (2002) go on to explain that competence builds on a foundation of basic clinical skills and scientific knowledge as well as moral development.

Competence, viewed from this comprehensive perspective, reveals the complex assemblage of knowledge, skills, attitudes, values, and ethics required in health service psychology that is the subject of clinical training and supervision. On the one hand, supervision must include broad foundational competencies, such as attention to relationship or self-assessment, whereas on the other hand, it simultaneously focuses on functional competencies, such as skills in conducting psychological assessment or treatment interventions, which are specific to the training objectives (Rodolfa et al., 2005).

Practically speaking, competence refers to a state of sufficiency relative to specific performance or training requirements within a given health care or training setting (Falender & Shafranske, 2004). Therefore, competence is not absolute nor an endpoint; it is always relative to the demands of the setting or context. Different health care settings (just as different patients or clients) require different competencies, and at times levels of ability, for treatment or supervision to be effective.

It is important to keep in mind (and to model to supervisees) that competence is constantly evolving and developing, such that practicing clinicians or supervisors never achieve absolute competence. For example, in our view, attaining licensure or board certification should never be considered a final destination; rather, it is one point along the way in a career, in which one strives for excellence, pushing competence forward to meet ever-changing clinical demands. Kaslow (personal communication, June 30, 2014) and other leaders in education and training now bemoan the use of the label, *competency movement* because for many the term implies that there is an endpoint to be achieved—a point at which one will be vested (for all time) as competent. The reality is that our own competence is fleeting because the field continuously advances knowledge and professional practices. It is also the case that we may face our own personal limitations as psychologists over the course of our careers. However, one benchmark of competence to which we all can aspire is the use of metacompetence, or reflection on what we do not know, which involves the ongoing self-assessment of capabilities and limitations, invites feedback from supervisors and trusted colleagues, and spurs us on to maintain and enhance competence. Clinical supervision is fertile ground for such an orientation to competence as a professional responsibility to take root.

An Intentional Framework

Competency-based clinical supervision aims to transform the training approach from reliance on assumptions of competence to demonstrations of competence. Although it is reasonable to expect that a supervisee will develop over a course of training, such an assumption is insufficient to establish competence. Similarly, whereas a supervisor may be well intentioned or talented as a clinician, such qualities do not guarantee competence as a supervisor. Measurable outcomes of clinical effectiveness and supervisory effectiveness are required to demonstrate competence. This involves commitment to carefully identify and assess the knowledge, skills, and attitudes that are assembled to form specific competencies. Rather than conducting global appraisals (or forming impressions) of competence, attention is directed to describe and evaluate the supervisee's (or supervisor's) specific use of knowledge, skills, and attitudes in observable behavioral terms. Implementation of this approach requires commitment and intention on the part of the supervisor (as well as the supervisee) because obtaining direct observations of discrete behavior requires not only focused attention but also the ability to assess accurately how each aspect is being used in the performance of the professional activity. A laissez-faire attitude, or even a well-intentioned but passive stance, toward clinical supervision will not suffice. Rather, an active, intentional, and engaged collaboration with the supervisee is required to carefully identify strengths and areas for development, provide feedback, and facilitate learning activities that enhance competence and instill professionalism. Adopting such a proactive stance encourages a vibrant and effective supervisory experience and provides a level of supervisory engagement ensuring client welfare.

COMPETENCY-BASED CLINICAL SUPERVISION

Competency-based clinical supervision (Falender & Shafranske, 2004, 2007) was developed to enhance the quality and effectiveness of supervision by providing a systematic and comprehensive approach to assess and develop specific clinical and supervision competencies and to perform the interrelated functions of observation, evaluation, feedback, and gatekeeping. The model is unique in its deliberative focus on the constituents of a specific competence as expressed in observable behavior and its focus on competence throughout the supervision and clinical training process. Competency-based clinical supervision is

> a metatheoretical approach that explicitly identifies the knowledge, skills, and attitudes and values that comprise clinical competencies, informs learning strategies and evaluation procedures, and meets criterion-referenced competence standards, consistent with evidence-based practices, regulations, and the local clinical setting. (APA, 2014, p. 5)

Competency-based clinical supervision is a meta- or transtheoretical approach that ensures accountability and is systematic in its orientation to the multiple competencies that comprise the art and science of supervision (e.g., Farber & Kaslow, 2010) and the development of clinical competence. It can be used in all forms of clinical training (e.g., psychotherapy, neuropsychology, assessment, behavioral health, school) and is suitable for use with a variety of psychotherapy orientations (Gonsalvez & Calvert, 2014), such as cognitive behavior therapy supervision. (Prototypes for transforming theory-based models to competency-based are available in a special issue of *Psychotherapy: Theory, Research, Practice, Training*, Volume 47, 2010, describing psychodynamic, cognitive behavior, humanistic–existential, systemic, and integrative theories.) Competency-based clinical supervision offers a systematic approach that readily accommodates the theoretical and artful aspects of the supervisor's unique skills and clinical orientation.

When we say *criterion-referenced* standards in the definition we gave earlier, we are referring to competencies that have been consensually agreed on by our profession, such as competency benchmarks (Fouad et al., 2009; Hatcher et al., 2013), the identification of the constituents of a competency through disassembling the competence into definable and potentially measurable units (i.e., specific knowledge, skills and attitudes, helps the supervisor and supervisee tailor methods of evaluation and training to the competency; Falender & Shafranske, 2004). Competencies are elements or components of competence, discrete knowledge, skills, and attitudes that comprise competence (Kaslow, 2004). Benchmarks are levels of competence consensually agreed to be appropriate for the developing stages of professional education and training in psychology (Fouad et al.,

2009). Such articulation allows for greater clarity in formulating training objectives and leads to more precise observations and targeted feedback, supporting supervisee development. Further, such an approach to competence informs every aspect of clinical training—the contents of the training rotation recruitment materials, criteria that are used in supervisee selection, method of evaluation, nature of feedback, competency-based learning processes, and associated activities. In addition, clear articulation of the competencies under training provides coherence in training and encourages transparency in supervision and training expectations.

BENEFITS OF COMPETENCY-BASED CLINICAL SUPERVISION

Among its strengths, we (Falender & Shafranske, 2012b) identified six major areas that are enhanced through the use of the model.

- Competency-based clinical supervision supports the development of the supervisory working alliance by articulating training goals and learning objectives. Supervisor and supervisee are more likely to be on the same page, minimizing confusion about the goals and tasks and enhancing their collaboration, which will contribute to establishing an effective working relationship.
- Competency-based clinical supervision supports the development of competence by identifying specific knowledge, skills, and attitudes and values required to form the competence. This orients the supervisor's observations and helps the supervisee to focus self-assessment and metacompetence on the competency in development.
- Competency-based clinical supervision supports formative and cumulative assessment by articulating the knowledge, skills, and attitudes that make up the competencies that are the focus of training. Such an approach minimizes confusion, eliminates final evaluation "surprises," and sets the supervisory agenda.
- Competency-based clinical supervision supports learning by identifying with specificity the areas for improvement. Supervisees are given useful feedback to orient experiential and other forms of learning.

Assessment, feedback, evaluation, and learning are clearly linked, and competence develops—which is encouraging for the supervisee and supervisor and further reinforces collaboration in the relationship.

- Competency-based clinical supervision supports an understanding of competence as a lifelong process and encourages career-long learning in which expertise continues to develop, which we assume enhances not only effectiveness but also satisfaction.
- Each of the aforementioned points, if faithfully implemented, supports the development of competence, and in so doing not only supports professional development but also ensures client welfare. Clients are well-served when supervisees, who are providing for their treatment under supervision, are oriented to always think in terms of the competencies that are required to provide the highest quality of care and supervisors are oriented to identify the knowledge, skills and attitudes, and values that must be demonstrated to support the client's welfare.

These predicted outcomes and benefits are logical and internally consistent with the procedures used and fit with our personal experiences in conducting supervision; however, further empirical research is needed to establish firmly the effectiveness of the approach.

HOW WE CAME TO A COMPETENCY-BASED MODEL OF CLINICAL SUPERVISION

Each of us was trained in an era in which little formal consideration was given to clinical supervision as a unique competence and, like our peers, we embarked on our supervisory journeys well-intentioned and drawing on appreciation of supervision as a learning process in which relationship played a central role, though we had no specific training. We individually cobbled together styles of supervision, focusing on enhancing supervisee self-awareness (what today we refer to as *metacompetence*) and incorporating a scientific attitude, focusing on the effectiveness of interventions. There were, of course, differences in our education and training experiences that influenced each of our approaches as well as the settings in which our professional lives took form.

I (Carol Falender) directed American Psychological Association–accredited internship programs at child and family community clinics for over 20 years (1978–2000). During the process, I assisted in and then wrote self-studies for accreditation. Throughout this experience, I viewed clinical supervision, a cornerstone of supervisee learning, professionalism, and development, as a sadly neglected aspect of clinical training. I trained practicum students, interns, and postdoctoral students in psychology. After I left the directorship role, I began focusing more intensely on clinical supervision, and with the support of my colleagues and friends at the California Psychological Association and Division II, Education and Training, of that association, I began organizing and conducting workshops on clinical supervision. I was influenced initially by the advanced scholarship in counseling psychology and, specifically, by Bernard and Goodyear (1998). Because my background was in child, adolescent, and family work, as well as clinical settings, I heard Paul Nelson speak of competency-based training and believed it was a missing link in supervision. I had worked with a highly diverse clinical population, across community and health center settings and was seeking a more applicable supervision model. I began to construct a framework related to competency-based supervision, drawing on my experience and the study and effort from self-studies for accreditation. I was fortunate to meet Edward Shafranske at this time through our work in the California Psychological Association and to collaborate with him on a workshop. He shared my passion for clinical supervision; he brought a wealth of knowledge, skills, attitudes, and perspective, and he proposed we write a book together. Our collaboration began in 2001 and has continued to the present. We were fortunate to be delegates to the Competencies Conference, and I was also a delegate to the Competencies Benchmarks Task Force, and through these, refined my thinking and learning through my association with incredible colleagues (Drs. Nadine Kaslow, Robert Hatcher, and Nadya Fouad, among others).

My (Edward Shafranske's) experiences as a faculty member (1988–present), director of clinical training (1995–1998), and PsyD program director (1998–present) at Pepperdine University strongly influenced my views on the importance of taking an explicit approach to competency-based graduate education and clinical training. In each of these roles, I was faced with the challenges inherent in translating academic learning experiences to professional competencies as well as in documenting student learning (for institutional review and accreditation self-studies). I came to integrate more completely experiential learning in the classroom (to complement lectures on clinical knowledge, theory, and research) and focused increased attention on knowledge in supervision (to complement reflective practice and skill development). Values were always an area of interest, and throughout my career I dedicated considerable time and scholarship to examining the interface of religion and spirituality in psychological treatment (for example, Shafranske, 1996, 2013, 2014). Although not identical to those interests, the role of attitudes and, more important, values in professional practice finds expression in our model of clinical supervision. In our view, values influenced by multiple cultural contexts and loyalties form important dispositions affecting professional commitment and practice as well as personal satisfaction. I find that the competency-based model is particularly useful in such specialized training. Finally, the opportunity to supervise a diversity of trainees, including first-year doctoral students, psychiatric residents, and highly experienced clinicians (in psychoanalytic training) reinforces the importance of carefully identifying and assessing competencies and facilitating collaborative processes, particularly with respect to the goals and means to achieve the goals of supervision.

Our collaboration initially took root in our mutual involvement in the California Psychology Association's Division II, Education and Training, which brought together leaders and practitioners from academic and clinical training institutions. Through presentations, conferences, and collaborative efforts, this organization fostered a commitment to ensure the highest quality of training throughout the state. A natural synergy emerged between us based on our shared commitment to the profession, to the principles of science-informed practice, and concern for the next generation of psychologists. Our approach to competency-based clinical supervision has also been informed by the contributions of many colleagues and leaders, such as Dr. Nadine Kaslow, who have inspired our efforts to advance professionalism and to prepare psychologists (and other health service professionals) to meet the clinical needs of clients and the community.

AN OVERVIEW OF THE CONTENTS OF THIS BOOK

The book is organized into two major sections: Foundations of Competency-Based Clinical Supervision, which presents the essential principles of the approach, and Core Competencies and Applications in Supervision, which highlights areas of specific supervisory focus. In Part I, Chapter 1 presents the groundwork and rationale for the model. In Chapter 2, we provide a blueprint for practice, describing each of the elements of competency-based clinical supervision and recommending best practices. In Chapter 3, we present an illustration of the approach through discussion of excerpts from a transcribed supervision session. In Part II, we focus attention on topics that are particularly salient to the conduct of clinical supervision, including diversity and multiculturalism (Chapter 4); personal factors (Chapter 5); legal, ethical, and regulatory competence (Chapter 6); supervisees who do not meet professional competence standards (Chapter 7); supervisor training and development (Chapter 8); and we close with a discussion of transforming supervision (Chapter 9).

IMPLEMENTING COMPETENCY-BASED
CLINICAL SUPERVISION

Implementing competency-based clinical supervision entails commitment and, consistent with the approach, requires specific knowledge, skills, and attitudes and values in its performance. Although this volume can furnish knowledge and present practical approaches to enhance supervision skills, the impetus to implement competency-based clinical supervision rests ultimately on your (our readers') attitudes, values-based commitments, and motivation. The commitment to be a competent and effective supervisor, to provide the highest quality of supervision, to transform supervision when necessary, to stretch one's abilities, or simply to become better informed about contemporary developments in clinical training and supervision attest to professionalism and the principles that animate our profession.

2

Implementing Competency-Based Clinical Supervision and Best Practices

Implementation of competency-based clinical supervision involves a multistep process that incorporates best practices and a structural framework. In this chapter, we present a blueprint for the structure and process of competency-based supervision that incorporates best practices and is based on theory and empirical research. We begin with a discussion of the knowledge, skills, and attitudes that constitute supervisor competence and the metafactors requisite for effective supervision, and we then go on to consider metacompetence, reflectivity, alliance, and the supervisory contract. The structure of supervision and its learning cycle are presented with consideration of multicultural, diversity, and personal factors; legal and ethical issues; professionalism; and self-care. Our discussion is informed by advances in theory and emerging empirical research (Bernard & Goodyear, 2014; Borders et al., 2014; Falender, Burnes, & Ellis, 2013; Falender, Ellis, & Burnes, 2013; Falender & Shafranske, 2004, 2007, 2014;

http://dx.doi.org/10.1037/15962-002
Supervision Essentials for the Practice of Competency-Based Supervision, by C. A. Falender and E. P. Shafranske

Foo Kune & Rodolfa, 2013; Inman et al., 2014; Ladany, Mori, & Mehr, 2013). We begin with an examination of the attitudes, values, and superordinate factors that influence the effectiveness of supervision.

ATTITUDES AND VALUES

Effective supervision is built on a foundation of personal and professional values and attitudes.[1] Whereas our primary focus is on the supervisor, we briefly consider the attitudes and competencies of supervisees that largely shape the supervision process. Supervisees who demonstrate genuine eagerness to learn; professional commitment; openness to feedback; personal characteristics of honesty, integrity, respect, and industry (to name a few); self-awareness; responsiveness to recommendations and directions; and sufficient clinical competence to learn and perform the clinical responsibilities in the training rotation contribute a large measure to the effectiveness of supervision (Falender & Shafranske, 2012b). Similarly, attitudes and values of supervisors directly affect supervisees and influence the process and effectiveness of supervision. Take a moment to reflect on those supervisors and supervisory experiences that had the most profound positive effects on your training and development. Attitudes and qualities that might have elicited include respect (including respect for personal boundaries), empathy, commitment to training (including the desire to be helpful and supportive), ethical conduct, professionalism, self-awareness, transparency, forthrightness, and clarity in expectations and efforts to provide accurate feedback.

On the basis of the literature and our experiences in consulting with supervisors, as well as conducting supervision and supervision of supervision, we identified four superordinate factors that we believe are particularly important and reflect the supervisor's values commitments (Falender & Shafranske, 2004). The first is *integrity-in-relationship*, which involves two components: (a) supervision that is complete—that is, all supervisory

---

[1]Both attitudes and values contribute to competence. *Attitudes* are cognitive appraisals that result in behavioral dispositions of varying strength; *values* include an attitudinal dimension, but may be seen as also involving an emotional component motivating behavior. Henceforth, we primarily use the term *attitude*, given its preferred use in the clinical supervision literature.

responsibilities (e.g., arranging regular meetings) are addressed and best practices are performed—and (b) supervision that is free from violations, such as boundary or other ethical violations, which mar the integrity of the supervisory relationship. Closely aligned with integrity-in-relationship, *ethical, values-based practice* underscores that ethics and values are constantly demonstrated and affect the supervisee. A supervisor's actions or the ethical climate of the training setting may have a greater impact than what is taught about ethics in courses. Third, *appreciation of diversity* expresses an attitude of inclusivity, respect for multiple diversity identities, individual differences and competence. Such appreciation extends to supervisory as well as clinical relationships and should permeate the training environment. Finally, *science-informed, evidence-based practice* reflects the values and perspectives of psychologists and is implemented by teaching supervisees how to use such practices and by supervisors using evidence-supported practices in clinical supervision. The supervisor's attention to these superordinate values, together with the principles enumerated in the American Psychological Association's (APA's; 2010) *Ethical Principles of Psychologists and Code of Conduct* (hereinafter, Ethics Code), not only strengthens the alliance and promotes the effectiveness of supervision but also models best practices of professional practice, influencing the supervisee's internalization of professionalism.

KNOWLEDGE

To conduct supervision effectively, supervisors must be highly knowledgeable about the scientific literature in all the clinical areas in which they are supervising, as well as the literature regarding clinical supervision, which informs their practice. Given the responsibilities of clinical management and ensuring patient welfare, supervisors must keep abreast of advances in the field. This is a tall order given the rapid increase of knowledge in which (a) the half-life of knowledge is 7 years, (b) the number of scientific publications doubles every 20 years, and (c) it takes about 17 years for the dissemination of empirically supported treatments from the research lab to practice (Balas & Boren, 2000).

It is likely that most supervisors completed their doctoral education and training before many of the empirically supported and "cutting edge" treatment protocols were developed. Supervisees may enter the training rotation with exposure to and/or training in these approaches and expect to use these clinical approaches, which poses a challenge for the supervisor—a competence gap. Fortunately, competence can be gained through reading, continuing education workshops, and consultation; however, the supervisor must still use metacompetence to determine whether their background is sufficient for them to supervise treatments in which they have limited training and experience or whether they have to identify alternative solutions for supervision (e.g., supervisee uses a different model, supervisee changes supervisors). Providing accurate and detailed information about the training program during student, intern, or fellow recruitment and within interviews lessens the chance of misunderstanding. The supervisor's clear description of rotation expectations and transparency about areas of competence ensures that supervisor and supervisee are in sync regarding the range of training opportunities.

Clinical supervision as a distinct competency includes a body of theoretical and empirical literature. Given the limited education and training many psychologists receive, supervisors may be limited in their knowledge of the field, leading to practices reflecting their own unique supervisory experiences or, in some form, "winging it." This volume and others (Bernard & Goodyear, 2014; Falender & Shafranske, 2004, 2008, 2012a, 2014; Milne, 2009), including the *Clinical Supervision Essentials* series (e.g., Sarnat, 2016), handbooks (Watkins & Milne, 2014), and journals (e.g., *Clinical Supervisor* and *Training and Education in Professional Psychology*), provide a foundation of information and perspectives on the conduct of clinical supervision. Psychologists conducting supervision should approach their competence as supervisors as they would any clinical specialty. Thoughtful self-reflection and self-assessment assists in identifying areas requiring further development of competence. Drawing on the scientific literature in directing and providing oversight of clinical work and in enhancing supervisory practice is consistent with the APA policy of evidence-based professional practice (APA Presidential Task Force on Evidence-Based Practice, 2006).

SKILLS

As presented in our definition (see Chapter 1), conducting clinical supervision involves a number of specific skills (see also Falender, Shafranske, & Ofek, 2014). These skill sets can be organized in relation to the three pillars that support the supervision process: relationship, inquiry, and educational or learning praxis (Falender & Shafranske, 2004). Strong interpersonal and communication skills, together with the aforementioned supervisor values (see Chapter 1) and attention to the power differential inherent in supervision, contribute to the development of an effective working relationship and play a role in the formation of the supervisory alliance. The ability to convey warmth, genuineness, and respect in addition to clear communications about expectations, assessment, feedback, and evaluation contribute to the alliance and the effectiveness of supervision. Although the supervisory relationship is a mutual creation, the supervisor bears primary responsibility for skillfully initiating a positive, supportive, and collaborative working relationship and setting the stage for the development of the supervisory alliance.

Inquiry serves two objectives: (a) eliciting information necessary to ensure adequate oversight and case management and (b) assisting the supervisee to develop or enhance self-awareness, metacompetence, and reflection on action. It takes skill to frame questions and to offer observations in a manner that facilitates reflectivity and accurate self-assessment, leading to effective self-monitoring and metacompetence. Supervisees learn how to observe and think about their clinical work in part by modeling the supervisor's approach to inquiry.

Educational or learning praxis aims to engage the supervisee in different processes of learning to ensure the development of competence. Rather than simply answering questions or giving directions, supervisors should use a variety of learning mechanisms, such as modeling, feedback, direct instruction, and self-regulated learning (Bearman et al., 2013; Milne, 2014), which we refer to as reflective and experiential practice. A number of skills are involved in guiding experiential learning, giving clear instructions, and facilitating self-awareness. We turn now to metafactors, which influence the supervisory alliance and supervision effectiveness.

COMPONENTS OF SUPERVISION EFFECTIVENESS

Although each element of supervision is important, certain components or structural metafactors have a significant and global impact on the supervisory experience and its effectiveness. We suggest that each element contributes individually to supervision outcome specific to the area addressed (e.g., attention to diversity in supervision affects supervisee attention to diversity when offering clinical services) and functions as a structural metafactor affecting supervision effectiveness generally. The following structural metafactors are essential to the integrity and effectiveness of supervision practice:

- metacompetence, self-assessment, and reflective practice;
- supervisory relationship and alliance (including identification and management of strains and ruptures);
- supervision contract (which ensures clarity and transparency in expectations);
- learning cycle (which systematically facilitates reflective practice, evaluation and feedback, and learning);
- infusion of consideration of multiculturalism and diversity of all participants anchored in the worldviews of the client(s);
- attention to personal factors;
- competence in legal and ethical standards, regulations (including ethical problem solving), and professionalism;
- evaluation and feedback;
- managing supervisees who do not meet competence standards; and
- self-care.

Each of these metafactors is discussed in this chapter (e.g., metacompetence, supervisory alliance) and/or addressed in greater depth in the remaining chapters (e.g., law and ethics, personal factors).

Metacompetence, Self-Assessment, and Reflective Practice

Metacompetence refers to the ability to know what one knows or does not know (Falender & Shafranske, 2007). On the surface, it may seem a simple or obvious task; however, closer examination reveals the inherent difficulty in identifying personal and professional shortcomings, such as a lacuna in our knowledge or skills or, particularly, how our interpersonal or supervisory style affects others. We may underestimate our talents, which limits our confidence, efficacy, and personal satisfaction. Accurate self-assessment is fundamental to the development of competence and is critically important to lifelong professional practice—when accountability is primarily vested in the psychologist as a licensed professional. Metacompetence is particularly important in clinical supervision, both in terms of establishing the learning agenda and in its development as a professional competency. Supervisees must develop self-reflectivity, an important competency benchmark, to accurately assess their clinical performance and identify areas to address in supervision to ensure patient welfare and to advance the training process. Similarly, supervisors use self-assessment to monitor continuously their effectiveness and pay attention to ways in which they might improve the supervisory relationship and training effectiveness.

Part of the transformation to competency-based supervision involves providing training in self-assessment for supervisors and supervisees alike. During the graduate trajectory, supervisees may assess themselves through objective ratings or by attending to inaccurate or erroneous rules. Although this may result in overconfidence among supervisees, it is also likely that following incorrect rules (Williams, Dunning & Kruger, 2013) and certain objective ratings may result in less competence. As such, collaboratively tracking competence development with their supervisors can address some of the supervisees' deficits in training, (Davis, Mazmanian, Fordis, Harrison, Thorpe, & Perrier, 2006; Dunning, Heath, & Suls, 2004). Thus, supervisors can anchor assessment, feedback, and goals using behavioral anchors based on the competency benchmarks (e.g., Fouad et al., 2009; Hatcher et al., 2013) and supplemented with competencies specific to the setting (e.g., child and family, neuropsychology, interdisciplinary practice). Because one of the major challenges in metacompetence is identifying what one does not know, benchmarks assist in this process by enumerating and describing competencies. Benchmark documents are invaluable in identifying competencies that may be "off the radar" and that may require deliberative development. Moreover, supervisors are also responsible for self-assessing on supervisory competencies (APA, 2014, 2015) by thoughtfully reviewing their knowledge, skills, and attitudes and obtaining feedback from supervisees and peers about their performance. They are also responsible for achieving reliability in assessing supervisees using the competency measures. The use of benchmarks and supervisor assessment is illustrated in more detail in Chapter 8.

The Supervisory Relationship: Alliance Formation and Repair

The supervisory alliance is fundamental to the practice of supervision and is considered the "quintessential integrative variable" (Watkins, 2014, p. 153) affecting the process and outcomes of clinical supervision, no matter the approach. By *supervisory alliance*, we are referring to the relationship between supervisor and supervisee in which the work of supervision takes place. It draws on the interpersonal strengths and personal and professional qualities of the supervisor, such as warmth, empathy, and expertise, to name a few. At the beginning, particular attention should be placed on processes that enhance the supervisory relationship. For example, it is important to attend to the power differential and to discuss the inherent conflicts in roles (i.e., duty to protect the public and to perform gatekeeping for the profession, so that unsuitable individuals do not enter). This can simultaneously enhance and support the professional development of the supervisee.

Part of alliance formation involves clarifying the expectations for supervision, assisting the supervisee in self-assessment of competence, and determining goals and tasks for the supervision process. This process is formalized in a written supervision contract (APA, 2014, 2015; Association of State and Provincial Psychology Boards, 2015; Falender & Shafranske, 2004), which we refer to as a *living supervision contract* because goals and tasks evolve and are updated with development of the supervisee. Through the process of goal and task development, an emotional bond forms between the supervisor and supervisee (Bordin, 1983), which is marked by trust, mutual respect, and collaboration. Launching directly into a discussion of clinical material while failing to establish an alliance presages problematic supervision (Falender & Shafranske, 2012b).

Although not discussed in Bordin's (1983) work, feminist psychologists address the power differential directly and transparently. For instance, balancing the power differential with the emotional bond is also viewed as an important part of establishing the alliance. Further, consistent with the views of feminist psychologists (Brown, 2016; Porter & Vasquez, 1997; Vargas, Porter, & Falender, 2008), we believe in the importance of promoting the valuing of supervisees, attending to structural barriers (e.g., roles and stereotypes), collaborative processes, client and student autonomy, and diverse multicultural perspectives. Typically, the supervisor holds not only power but also significant privilege (perhaps by education, job, diversity identities, for example) in the relationship. These aspects of privilege frequently not addressed in clinical supervision are a major factor in the supervisee–supervisor relationship and in the assessment, intervention, and general assumptions made about the client. Initiating a respectful process and not requiring disclosures from the supervisee about areas unrelated to client process or treatment while also adopting a reflective, open, and curious stance is a critical aspect of establishment of the supervisory alliance.

In supervisory relationships (as in human relationships more generally), it is likely that strains will occur. These may be caused by conflicts between supervisor and supervisee with respect to supervision goals or means to achieve the goals, inadequate attention to diversity, poor interpersonal skills, lack of clinical supervisory competence, inadequate supervision, lack of institutional support, and the pressure and frustrations inherent in clinical work (particularly in understaffed institutions). Ruptures, forms of strain imperiling or foreclosing the alliance, are likely to follow breaches of ethics and boundary crossings (sexual and professional) and may constitute harmful supervision (Ellis et al., 2014) if the ruptures are not repaired. Given the power differential, supervisees often do not directly convey dissatisfaction or strains to their supervisor. Supervisors should be mindful of signs of strain (e.g., changes in supervisee disclosure and engagement) and discuss how strains may occur at the beginning of the course of supervision, both normalizing and offering suggestions on how supervisor and supervisee might both work to address potential differences and misattunement. If a marker of strain is observed, the supervisor should wait initially to see whether the relationship self-corrects; if not, the supervisor should reflect on his or her possible contributions to the apparent strain, acknowledge these to the supervisee, and respectfully encourage exploration. However, again due to the power differential, supervisees are likely to deny that a strain exists or may minimize any impact ("Everything is fine"); the supervisor should not (in our view) challenge the supervisee (because this would likely exacerbate the existing strain) but should reflect on behavioral change, such as decreased disclosure in supervision. If after a few sessions the supervisee is still not fully participating in supervision, the poor performance should be addressed as such. It is often useful to seek advice or consultation at this point regarding possible interventions or, in some instances, to determine whether a change in supervisory responsibilities would be appropriate.

The Supervision Contract

The supervision contract is at the heart of supervision and defines and describes each of the elements and processes (e.g., goals, structure of supervision, expectations of supervisees and supervisors) that will inform supervision. Significant attention has been directed to outlining the logistical aspects of the contract, including expectations, requirements, and contingencies (Thomas, 2010). However, in competency-based supervision, the contract is "living"—it evolves with the development of the supervisee. That is, the contract is structured on the supervisee's self-assessment and the ongoing supervisor feedback based on live or video observation, video review, and/or supervision discussion and considers as well the effectiveness of the supervision, including expectations and processes. The orientation is always toward competence, using the competency benchmarks to revise or refocus training objectives on achieving specific behaviorally anchored competencies and assessing the effectiveness of supervision.

Goals

Goals are derived from the supervisee's self-assessment (using benchmarks or a relevant specialty competency frame), input, feedback, and the collaboratively agreed on current competence of the supervisee and plans for future development. The goals and tasks are measurable. These are reviewed in each supervision session and revised collaboratively as they are achieved.

Means to Achieve the Goals

In addition to describing the goals, the supervision dyad planfully and through consensus identifies means to achieve the goal. This includes highlighting the specific supervisee, supervisor, and dyadic processes entailed. We emphasize that these goals and means are not immutable but rather evolve and are amended or changed over the course of supervision. For example, if the supervisee were to have a designated goal of "Describes how others experience him/her and identifies roles one might play within a group" (Fouad et al., 2009, Table 1 A, p. 4) and the dyad concludes on the basis of planned self-report, observation, and the supervision process that significant progress has been made, the next defined goal might be "Monitors and evaluates attitudes, values, and beliefs towards diverse others" (Fouad et al., 2009, Table 1 A, p. 4). Development and assessment of this competency involves a similar process of mutually identifying performance of such in supervision and observed client work. Each supervisee addresses two to three goals at a given time, building on the progress achieved. The supervisor's role, designated as a task, is to provide feedback, model reflection, and address client progress and attention to the treatment model, interventions, and client response. Failure to consistently attend to specific performance benchmarks (by relying solely on assumptions of competence) may result in the oft-cited supervision error of inadequately evaluating the supervisee's competence, which compromises the supervisor's "entrustability" of the supervisee (Sterkenburg, Barach, Kalkman, Gielen, & ten Cate, 2010). Specifically, it questions the supervisor's assessment of what clinical responsibilities and level of difficulty he or she can entrust to the supervisee as a clinician.

Structure and Parameters of Supervision

Exhibit 2.1 contains a comprehensive outline of the elements of the contract and Exhibit 2.2 is a sample supervision contract template. Formal

Exhibit 2.1

Elements of the Supervision Contract

Priorities of Supervision

Monitor and ensure welfare and protection of patients of the
supervisee

Be a gatekeeper for the profession to ensure that only competent
professionals enter

Promote the development of the supervisee's competence and
professional identity

Provide evaluative feedback to the supervisee and facilitate learning
processes to enhance competence

Promote the development of the supervisee's competence and
professional identity

Training institution location(s), days, and hours services provided

Length of contract period with end date

Provisions for vacations, holidays, religious observances, medical
leave

Legal and Ethical Requirements

Informed consent to supervision

Maintenance of indemnity or malpractice insurance, if required

Confidentiality in clinical practice and limits of confidentiality in
supervision

Maintaining clinical charts and supervision logs (supervisor) and
access to those

Adherence to laws, regulations, and standards of practice, including specific ethical codes of conduct, including, for example,
mandated reporting requirements and the training institution's
policies and procedures regarding the Americans With
Disabilities Act

Adherence to federal, state, and local laws and regulations (e.g.,
Health Insurance Portability and Accountability Act and Family
Educational Rights and Privacy Act, if required)

Exhibit 2.1

Elements of the Supervision Contract (*Continued*)

Adherence to the training institution or setting personnel policies and regulations

Expectation that personal experience is an important part of clinical supervision (APA, 2010, 7.04)

Supervisor–supervisee–client boundaries generally and specific to setting

Clarification of responsibilities of primary supervisor, delegated supervisors, director of training, and other supervisors (as applicable)

Procedures to address clinical emergencies (including procedures to contact supervisor and backup supervisors)

Clinical Performance Expectations

Specific competencies to be developed (with discussion of the knowledge, skills, and values and attitudes assembled to form the competency)

Hours of direct and other services to be provided

Performance expectations and benchmarks of developing competence

Professionalism (as per training institution and profession standards)

Roles and Expectations of Supervisee and Supervisor

Role and responsibilities of supervisor (responsibilities to client; case management; overseeing professional services provided by supervisee; responsibilities to supervisee, profession, and public)

Role and responsibilities of supervisee (responsibilities to clients, supervisor, training institution)

Supervision Process

Organization (format, frequency, length of supervision sessions)

Mutually defined goals and tasks of supervision

Content (knowledge, skills, values assembled to form competency)

(continues)

Exhibit 2.1

Elements of the Supervision Contract (*Continued*)

Attention to diversity and contextual factors regarding (or with respect to) client, the therapeutic process, and supervision

Attention to personal factors (responsiveness, reactivity; i.e., countertransference, bias) affecting the therapeutic process and supervision

Structure of the supervision session (preparation for supervision, in-session structure and processes, feedback, follow-up)

Learning activities

Distinctions between supervisor comments, recommendations, and directives (actions which the supervisee is required to perform)

Attention to strains in supervisory relationship and discussion of mutual feedback to enhance the supervisory relationship and its effectiveness

Notification of areas in which supervisee is not meeting performance competence standards

Observation, Evaluation, and Feedback Procedures

Expectation of supervisee self-assessment, attention to metacompetence, and use of reflective practices

Approaches to observe supervisee professional performance (live supervision, video or audio recordings, transcription, experience sampling of recordings, self-report)

Modes of formative and summative evaluation (contents, format, dates of summative reports, incorporation of response or comments by supervisee)

Possibility that cases will be transferred or supervisor will join supervisee as co-therapist if it is beyond supervisee competence and/or is judged to be in the best interest of the client

Discussion of what constitutes failure to meet performance competence criteria, including distinctions between normative developmental challenges and poor performance, requiring a remediation plan

---

Exhibit 2.1

Elements of the Supervision Contract (*Continued*)

Processes for formal remediation, probation, and termination
Possibility that supervisee will be referred for personal therapy
   because supervision is distinct from personal psychotherapy
Means to provide feedback to the supervisor
Complaint and resolution processes

Note. Adapted from *APA Handbook of Clinical Psychology: Vol. 5. Education and Profession* (p. 183) by J. C. Norcross, G. R. VandenBos, and D. K. Freedheim (Eds.), 2016, Washington, DC: American Psychological Association. Copyright 2016 by the American Psychological Association.

Exhibit 2.2

Sample Supervision Contract Template

I. *Priorities of Supervision*
- Monitor and ensure welfare and protection of patients of the supervisee.
- Be a gatekeeper for the profession to ensure competent professionals enter.
- Promote development of supervisee's professional identity and competence.
- Provide evaluative feedback to the supervisee.

Content and Context of Supervision

II. *Structure of Supervision*
- The primary supervisor during this training period will be _____, who will provide _____ hours of supervision per week. The delegated supervisor(s) during this training period will be _____, who will provide _____ hours of supervision per week. Additional supervision will be ____ Group.

(continues)

Exhibit 2.2

Sample Supervision Contract Template (*Continued*)

- Structure of the supervision session: supervisor and supervisee preparation for supervision, in-session structure and processes, live or video observation ____ times per ____ (time period).
- Limits of confidentiality exist for supervisee disclosures in supervision (e.g., supervisor normative reporting to graduate programs, licensing boards, training teams, program directors, upholding legal and ethical standards).

III. *Duties and Responsibilities of Supervisor*
- Assumes legal responsibility for services offered by the supervisee.
- Oversees and monitors all aspects of patient case conceptualization and treatment planning, assessment, and intervention, including but not limited to emergent circumstances, duty to warn and protect, legal, ethical, and regulatory standards (including Americans With Disabilities Act, Health Insurance Portability and Accountability Act, and Family Educational Rights and Privacy Act, diversity factors, management of supervisee reactivity or countertransference to patient, strains to the supervisory relationship.
- Upholds training institution's organizational and institutional rules, policies, and procedures.
- Ensures availability when the supervisee is providing client or patient services.
- Reviews and signs off on all reports, case notes, and communications.
- Develops and maintains a respectful and collaborative supervisory relationship within the power differential.
- Practices effective supervision that includes describing supervisor's theoretical orientations for supervision and therapy, and maintaining a distinction between supervision and psychotherapy. Assists the supervisee in setting and attaining goals.
- Provides feedback anchored in supervisee training goals, objectives, and competencies.

Exhibit 2.2

Sample Supervision Contract Template (*Continued*)

- Provides ongoing formative and end-of-supervisory-relationship summative evaluation on forms available at _____ (website or training manual).
- Informs supervisee when the supervisee is not meeting competence criteria for successful completion of the training experience and implements remedial steps to assist the supervisee's development. Guidelines for processes that may be implemented should competencies not be achieved are available at (website or training manual).
- Discloses training, licensure including number and state(s), areas of specialty and special expertise, previous supervision training and experience, and areas in which he or she has previously supervised.
- Reschedules sessions to adhere to the legal standard and the requirements of this contract if the supervisor must cancel or miss a supervision session.
- Maintains documentation of the clinical supervision and services provided.
- If the supervisor determines that a case is beyond the supervisee's competence, the supervisor may join the supervisee as cotherapist or may transfer a case to another therapist, as determined by the supervisor to be in the best interest of the patient.
- Inform of maintenance of indemnity or malpractice insurance, if required.

IV. *Duties and Responsibilities of the Supervisee*
- Understands the responsibility of the supervisor for all supervisee professional practice and behavior.
- Follows the training institution's organizational and institutional rules, policies and procedures.
- Implements supervisor directives, and discloses clinical issues, concerns, and errors as they arise.

(continues)

Exhibit 2.2

Sample Supervision Contract Template (*Continued*)

- Identifies to patients his or her status as supervisee, the name of the clinical supervisor, and describes the supervisory structure (including supervisor access to all aspects of case documentation and records) obtaining patient's informed consent to discuss all aspects of the clinical work with the supervisor.

- Attends supervision prepared to discuss patient cases with completed case notes and case conceptualization, patient progress, clinical and ethics questions, and literature on relevant evidence-based practices.

- Informs supervisor of clinically relevant information from patient, including patient progress, risk situations, self-exploration, supervisee emotional reactivity, or counter-transference to patient(s).

- Integrates supervisor feedback into practice and provides feedback weekly to supervisor on patient and supervision process.

- Seeks out and receives immediate supervision on emergent situations. Supervisor contact information: _____
  _____.

- If the supervisee must cancel or miss a supervision session, the supervisee will reschedule the session to ensure adherence to the legal standard and this contract.

- A formal review of this contract will be conducted on: _____ when a review of the specific goals (described below) will be made.

- We, _____ (supervisee) and _____ (supervisor), agree to follow the parameters described in this supervision contract and to conduct ourselves in keeping with the American Psychological Association Ethical Principles and Code of Conduct or the Canadian Psychological Association Code of Ethical Conduct.

  Supervisor: _____ Date: _____

  Supervisee: _____ Date: _____

Exhibit 2.2

Sample Supervision Contract Template (*Continued*)

Dates contract is in effect: Start date: _____ End date: _____

Mutually determined goals and tasks by supervisor and supervisee to accomplish (and updated on completion).

Goal 1:

    Task for supervisee

    Task for supervisor

Goal 2:

    Task for supervisee

    Task for supervisor

Note. The authors would like to express their appreciation to Drs. Emil Rodolfa and Jack Schaffer for their input in the development of the supervision contract. Copyright 2014 by Carol A. Falender. Reprinted with permission.

---

elements include clarification of the highest duties of the supervisor: the legal and ethical responsibilities of protection of the public and gatekeeping for the profession, which creates a tension with the supervisor's other major duty of fostering the development and enhancing the competence of the supervisee. The contract also includes setting specific expectations—performance criteria for the training or employment site and consequences if those are not met—expectations that supervisees' personal reactions to clients and personal exploration are normative parts of supervision and all clinical activity. Such exploration (as previously disclosed to supervisees at application to the site per the Ethics Code; APA, 2010, Standard 7.04) includes management of countertransference and repair of strains and ruptures to the supervisory relationship. Also included is specific attention to defining the distinct limits of confidentiality. These include the supervisory responsibility and ethical and legal mandate to disclose supervisee information to graduate schools, training committees, site supervision teams and faculty, and licensing boards and the responsibility to uphold legal and ethical standards, limiting the confidentiality of personal or private disclosures supervisees make to supervisors because of the multiple duties of the supervisor (e.g., gatekeeping and protection of the client).

The issue of confidentiality is frequently misunderstood because supervisees often believe that personal disclosures they make to the supervisor will be held confidential and that when supervisors share such disclosures, it is a supervisory ethical infraction (Ladany, Lehrman-Waterman, Molinaro, & Wolgast, 1999; Wall, 2009). Supervisors should discuss the proper and sensitive use of supervisee disclosures and clarify the limits of confidentiality at the beginning and when appropriate during the course of supervision to avoid misunderstanding. Lack of disclosure in the supervisory relationship is potentially a significant problem because supervisors rely on supervisee disclosure sometimes exclusively, but ideally to supplement their direct observations of supervisee performance.

Expectations of the Supervisee

Performance expectations of the supervisee are clearly and comprehensively described and linked to a competencies document, such as that containing benchmarks (Fouad et al., 2009; Hatcher et al., 2013), and to the training program's handbook or site personnel practices (if available). Such clarity in expectations sets the training agenda, enhances transparency, encourages collaboration, and aims to avoid strains based on misalignment of expectations and responsibilities.

The expectations regarding preparation for supervision sessions are clarified; these include completion of case record keeping and documentation, video review, supervisee preparation of formulations, research on treatment options, and questions to be discussed. Emergencies are defined regarding the setting and proper procedures for dealing with these are outlined, including mechanisms for supervisor contact. Specific topics that require supervision (e.g., child and elder abuse reporting, homicidality, suicidality) are described, including reference to the legal standards of the jurisdiction or context regarding duty to warn and protect and how to reach the supervisor in those instances. The contract also describes the expectation that supervisors will introduce ethical decision-making models to address the multiple ethical dilemmas that arise in supervision and the clinical process (e.g., Koocher & Keith-Spiegel, 2008). Normative multiple relationships between supervisors and supervisees and supervisees/ therapists and clients may be described with ethical decision-making frames for determining whether to engage in the relationship (Gottlieb, Robinson, & Younggren, 2007). Clarity about boundaries and setting-specific expectations are described. What is normative in certain settings may be inappropriate or prohibited in others. Clarity that supervision is not psychotherapy is essential. Due to the concern that much of the supervisee's training in ethics may have been in one course with a focus on risk avoidance or risk management, the contract lays out the expectation that ethical practice and identification of ethical issues or dilemmas are significant competencies in supervision (Falender & Shafranske, 2014).

Expectations of the Supervisor and the Supervision Process

Expectations of the supervisor and the process of supervision, with particular attention to evaluation and feedback, are discussed. In addition to the training program's performance expectations, it is important for supervisors to present an overview of their approach to supervision, including their assumptions about training, their preferred supervisory approach, procedures to be used in observing the supervisee's clinical work (e.g., live supervision, videotape review), and their approach to evaluation and feedback, including performance expectations, benchmarks of competence, tools used in evaluation and feedback, use of formative feedback and nature of summative feedback, review of confidentiality, learning and training approaches, and the expectation that both supervisor and supervisee will engage in processes of assessment and feedback to enhance the effectiveness of supervision.

The Learning Cycle

With the establishment of a developing supervisory alliance, a measure of trust, and mutual understanding of supervision parameters and expectations discussed in the contract, the learning process commences.[2] Supervision involves cycles of performance (i.e., supervisees perform clinical

---

[2] This model is based in part on the experiential-learning cycle (Kolb, 1984) of experimenting, experiencing, reflecting, conceptualizing, and planning, as applied to supervision (Milne, 2009, 2014).

services for the benefit of clients), observation (i.e., supervisee and supervisor, individually and jointly in supervision, observe clinical interaction focusing on the knowledge, skills, and attitudes assembled to form the competence), reflection (i.e., supervisee and supervisor, individually and jointly in supervision, reflect on their observations and construct an understanding of the clinical experience as related to the therapeutic process, the treatment plan and goals, and the associated competencies), evaluation/assessment/feedback (i.e., supervisor encourages supervisee self-assessment and provides feedback, including evaluative and summative comments), and planning (i.e., identifies interventions and assesses their effectiveness). Each aspect is important to the whole process and effectiveness of supervision; however, a critical responsibility is obtaining sufficient knowledge of the supervisee's clinical work (by direct observation and supervisee disclosure) to ensure the effectiveness of the professional services performed by the supervisee. Supervisors may mistakenly rely totally on supervisee recall, which is affected by relationship variables, especially in light of the hierarchical nature of the supervisory relationship. The learning cycle progresses with special attention to the competencies under development as identified by the benchmarks and in the living supervision contract. Each element in the cycle identifies and addresses the knowledge, skills, and attitudes involved in the clinical service; orients observation, evaluation and feedback to such; and develops learning and intervention plans specific to the constituents of the competency (see Figure 2.1).

Multiculturalism and Diversity

Multicultural competence is critical to competent and ethical practice (APA Presidential Task Force on Evidence-Based Practice, 2006; Vasquez, 2014). It is integral to evidence-based practice (APA Presidential Task Force on Evidence-Based Practice, 2006) and is a competency benchmark (Fouad et al., 2009) in both clinical practice and supervision (APA, 2015). Supervisors have to be particularly cognizant and intentional to infuse consideration of diversity throughout supervision by, for example, attending to the multicultural identities and contexts affecting the supervisory relationship and process. Failure to attend to these features in supervision

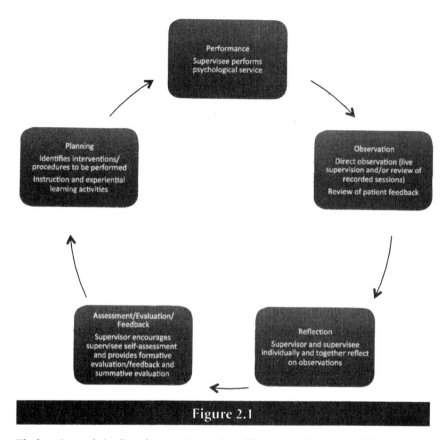

Figure 2.1

The learning cycle in clinical supervision. Adapted from *APA Handbook of Clinical Psychology: Vol. 5. Education and Profession* (p. 185) by J. C. Norcross, G. R. VandenBos, and D. K. Freedheim (Eds.), 2016, Washington, DC: American Psychological Association. Copyright 2016 by the American Psychological Association.

places in peril the supervisory alliance and compromises the effectiveness of supervision (see Chapter 4, this volume, for further discussion).

Personal Factors

Personal as well as professional factors influence professional practice. Attitudes, beliefs, and values; interpersonal style; and emotional sensitivity (to name a few) originating in experiences outside of clinical training often influence the conduct of treatment and supervision. Supervision provides the context for the exploration of such factors and monitors their impact on client welfare and the supervisory process. Attention to personal factors, akin to consideration of multicultural identities, contributes to clinical and supervisory competence. (See Chapter 5 for further discussion and Chapter 3 for an illustration.)

Legal and Ethical Competencies and Professionalism

Supervision aims to assist the supervisee in developing competence in ethical and legal practice and decision making. Ethical practice and compliance with legal requirements are essential and are embedded in professionalism. Supervision contributes to the development of professionalism by setting clear expectations for comportment and ethical practice; however, the greatest impact is likely found in the supervisor's actions. The "hidden curriculum" in training occurs through the intentional and unintended modeling that takes place throughout the training setting at all times (see Chapter 6).

Evaluation and Feedback

Determining the content of evaluation is central to the process. Articulation of specific training goals and competencies and their behavioral benchmarks (in the contract) provides direction to the process of evaluation and informs the focus of the feedback to be given. The benchmarks (Fouad et al., 2009) provide an excellent framework, with behavioral indicators and a broad range of competencies, both foundational and functional, on which to structure observations and conduct evaluation. Use of live observation with targeted goals and feedback is the highest standard and provides the most accurate and helpful feedback and assessment data. It also meets criteria for feedback being given close in time to the event and has great specificity because the supervisee and supervisor can observe together. Other frameworks for evaluation and systematic feedback include Milne's (2008) Trainee Competence Checklist and the Therapist Evaluation Checklist (Hall-Marley, 2004, cited in Falender & Shafranske, 2004, Appendix L).

The evaluation process not only involves evaluative feedback provided by the supervisor but also incorporates supervisee self-assessment, encouraging metacompetence and reflective practice.

Relatedly, Sobell, Manor, Sobell, and Dum (2008) described a technique akin to motivational interviewing in which the supervisee reviews his or her tape of the clinical session and considers what could be done differently. This summary is then brought to supervision. Self-assessment of competence related to clinical work is a component of one of the major techniques of competence assessment, the Objective Structured Clinical Exam format, in which a standardized patient is the subject of a videotaped intake assessment as a measure of competence (Logie, Bogo, Regehr, & Regehr, 2013).

Supervisors bear the responsibility for monitoring and providing feedback and evaluation to supervisees, ensuring that clarity is achieved in informing the supervisee if he or she is not meeting performance criteria with remediation of identified competence areas. Consistent with this responsibility, establishing a "timely and specific process for feedback" (APA, 2010, Standard 7.06(a)) and "evaluation on the basis of their actual performance on relevant and established program requirements" (APA, 2010, Standard 7.06(b)) are ethical standards. Assessment, evaluation, and formative feedback should be given in each supervision session and should be anchored in behavioral terms and be specific to knowledge, skills, and attitudes. Feedback should be precise and given in a manner that leads to the development of learning strategies on which to enhance competence (see Exhibit 2.3). The process should be a respectful one in which the supervisor models respect for the supervisee and the supervisee responds in kind. Evaluative information given in summative evaluations, such as mid-year evaluations, should never be a surprise. Rather, such evaluations reflect a culmination of ongoing assessment, evaluation, and feedback processes, anchored in competencies benchmarks and set forth in the contract. Summative feedback presents the course of training and supervision, details the progression in the supervisee's development of competence, describes the present state of competence development, and sets the agenda for future training and advancement.

Exhibit 2.3

Giving Effective Feedback

1. Before giving feedback, invite the supervisee to self-reflect on his or her performance and engage in self-assessment, which will contribute to the development of metacompetence. Building on the supervisee's accurate self-assessment and openness to reflective practice enhances openness to supervisor feedback.

2. Prepare to give feedback by linking observations to the specific assessed area of competence and/or professionalism under development and assess whether the supervisee's performance meets expectations, exceeds expectations, or is below expectations. If the supervisee's behavior or attitude is below performance expectations, assess whether this reflects a normative developmental challenge (a performance difficulty often observed in training that ordinarily is remedied by feedback and direction) or is associated with other areas of poor performance that require formal remediation.

3. Provide a framework for the feedback that (a) communicates the importance of the competence issue to be addressed; (b) identifies the developmental level (e.g., "normative" developmental challenge, exceeds performance expectations, or does not meet performance expectations); (c) while giving corrective feedback, provides examples that illustrate behaviors or attitudes that meet performance expectations; and (d) infuses the giving of evaluative comments as constructive criticism by suggesting avenues for improvement (i.e., how to make improvements), perhaps by building on perceived strengths and offers of assistance.

4. Give clear feedback. The most effective feedback is that which
   - is specific (behaviorally anchored),
   - delineates the knowledge, skills, and attitudes and values that require attention,
   - frames competence with a developmental orientation,

Exhibit 2.3

Giving Effective Feedback (*Continued*)

- acknowledges strengths through which competence will be enhanced,
- invites reflection and articulation of specific areas for development, and
- leads to discussion of learning strategies, including learning in the supervision session.

5. Invite the supervisee to share whether the feedback appears to be accurate and add any comments.
6. Give assessment and feedback that are formative and continuous and that will contribute to the summative evaluation.

Commitment to these practices ensures that the supervisee is provided with the requisite ongoing assessment, evaluation, monitoring and feedback necessary for case management and professional development. However, it appears that in many supervisory relationships, the standards of consistent, ongoing formative evaluation and feedback are not met. This compromises both client welfare and supervisee development and strains the supervisory alliance. Supervisees report that lack of supervisor monitoring is an ethical infraction (Ladany et al., 1999; Wall, 2009). It is imperative that supervisors provide corrective and evaluative feedback to supervisees when competence issues first arise. Supervisors may hesitate, believing the inadequate performance is a "developmental" issue or that the supervisee is not "ready" to receive such feedback. Those are not good reasons to withhold evaluative information from the supervisee. In addition to evaluation and feedback regarding clinical competence, the effectiveness of supervision should also be assessed, incorporating formative and summative models of assessment, evaluation, and feedback. Two-way feedback occurs from supervisor to supervisee in every supervision session and from supervisee to supervisor concerning the perceived efficacy of the supervision processes.

Self-Care

Self-care is an ethical imperative for supervisors and supervisees alike. In the APA Ethics Code, Principle A (APA, 2010), "Psychologists strive to be aware of the possible effect of their own physical and mental health on their ability to help those with whom they work," and Standard 2.06 of the Code (2.06(a) and (b), APA, 2010) describe personal problems and conflicts describing self awareness steps—becoming aware of personal problems, knowing (or they should know) that there is a substantial likelihood that their personal problems will prevent them from performing competently. Modeling self-care is an important supervisory responsibility.

Emotional competence, then, refers to self-awareness of the status of one's functioning—the impact of professional and personal events on one's ability to remain empathically engaged. This includes awareness of one's abilities, competencies, and limitations and the factors, situations, and presentations that evoke emotional responses. Social, cultural, and political factors weigh in significantly. We have to remain mindful that the same essential empathic engagement, including feeling the client's pain and trauma, increases the risk of vicarious traumatization.

Psychologists emerging from graduate training often find it difficult to remember the kinds of leisure activities that sustained them previously. In a professional roles course the first author (CF) teaches, students report that the intensity of graduate school leaves no time for many pleasures such as music, dance, reading, sports, physical exercise, yoga, mindfulness, or any of a whole realm of activities that would potentially be buffers against vicarious traumatization, emotional exhaustion, and burnout. And the situation is exacerbated by the student's immersion into doing therapy, which is full time, intimate, confidential, and nonreciprocal (APA, 2014, 2015). Supervisors have a multiple complex relationship with self-care: They urge supervisees to engage in it to remain healthy, but they also want supervisees to be maximally productive, take on new cases and activities, and work many hours. Also, supervisors do not necessarily foresee the impact on supervisees of full-time clinical work and client disclosures of highly traumatic material that may elicit intense emotional responses; supervisees may not be forthcoming in disclosing such an impact. Further, productivity demands on staff have diminished the amount of time colleagues could spend having informal conversations or providing collegial support to each other to balance the high levels of exposure to stress, conflict, and pain of the clients, thus increasing isolation. Supervisees may be in a setting with only traumatic exposure clients (e.g., those exposed to child abuse, sexual abuse, posttraumatic stress disorder), with no option for seeing a range of clients, which could be a protective factor against burnout. Pope (1994) described the combination of high stress and the misconception that psychologists should be invulnerable as a conspiracy of silence.

How may supervisors make self-care more accessible, and not simply another activity to be added to an already overfull supervisee's schedule? Johnson, Barnett, Elman, Forrest, and Kaslow (2013) and Johnson and colleagues (2014) proposed creating a communitarian culture/community of competence, a concept that will be powerful for supervisors to model and instill in supervisees. They proposed the development of a culture of authenticity and self-awareness, with the potential for supervisors to model self-assessment, authenticity, and nondefensiveness. The model is described further in Chapter 9.

Intentionality and Deliberative Practice

Implementing competency-based clinical supervision requires both intentionality and deliberative practice on the part of the supervisor. An emerging body of literature on expertise in fields such as music and medicine has suggested that deliberative practice leads to high levels of performance (Chow et al., 2015). We speculate that some of the same principles and practices that advance expertise in these fields are involved in supervisor effectiveness. In our view, the starting point is to hold to the intention to conduct competency-based clinical supervision and to fully implement each of the elements of the model. Second, the knowledge, skills, and attitudes of the supervisor in the conduct of supervision can be purposefully developed and enhanced. Supervisor competence can be advanced through deliberate, systematic, and purposeful implementation of the designated practices (e.g., alliance formation, attention to personal factors).

However, routine performance of a particular skill through repetition is not enough to lead to improvement. What appears necessary are specific training activities that target (in our approach) specific knowledge, skills and attitudes, continuous and deliberate practice of the model, and conscious monitoring of outcomes and feedback carried out over extended periods of time. As in clinical competence, the development of supervision competence requires clear articulation of the knowledge, skills, and attitudes assembled to form the competence and participation in a learning cycle that involves self and other observations, evaluations, feedback, and metacompetence.

3

Illustration: Excerpt From a Transcript of a Supervisory Session

In this chapter, we present excerpts from a transcript of a supervision session recorded for the *Competency-Based Supervision* DVD (American Psychological Association [APA], 2016) to illustrate some of the features of our approach. We also include discussion of aspects of previous supervision meetings, which informed the supervisory process as a whole and set the stage for the work in the session.

THE SUPERVISEE

At the time of the DVD taping, Traci[1] was a doctoral student in an APA-accredited clinical psychology program and was supplementing her external practicum rotations by conducting treatment in one of the university's

---

[1] Excerpted dialogue and other information from Traci Bank's supervision session with Dr. Edward Shafranske is reprinted with permission.

http://dx.doi.org/10.1037/15962-003
Supervision Essentials for the Practice of Competency-Based Supervision, by C. A. Falender and E. P. Shafranske

outpatient community clinics. Having obtained training in cognitive behavior therapy (CBT) and dialectical behavior therapy (DBT), she was seeking supervision to expand her competence in providing psychodynamic psychotherapy, which was an approach in which she had a strong interest and some previous exposure and training. The supervision consisted of weekly 90-minute sessions over a 2-year period and was conducted in a group setting with additional individual appointments as appropriate to clinical management and specialized training.

THE SUPERVISOR

The supervisor (EPS) was a faculty member and director of the doctoral program in which Traci was enrolled. He had a particular interest in the theoretical and applied integration of multiple models of treatment and the use of empirically supported treatments, including psychoanalytic-informed protocols, such as transference-focused psychotherapy and mentalization-based therapy in the context of training and clinical supervision.

THE SUPERVISORY PROCESS

The supervision was conducted integrating the principles presented in this volume. Particularly relevant to the session under discussion was attention to personal factors, which were explicitly addressed in the supervision contract through informed consent and clarity about expectations, and obtaining consensus about the training objectives and the means to achieve the goals (see Chapters 2 and 5). Consideration was also given to the alliance and impacts of the multiple roles of the supervisor (administrator, faculty instructor, supervisor) and supervisee (student, clinical trainee)—for instance, the effects of clinical supervision on classroom performance and vice versa.

THE TREATMENT UNDER SUPERVISION

In brief, the treatment consisted of individual psychotherapy with a man presenting with significant and long-standing difficulties in interpersonal relations and vulnerability in the regulation of intense emotional states, impulses, and self-esteem, consistent with the diagnosis of borderline personality disorder. The fundamental approach to treatment was psychodynamic in nature based in part on the principles of transference-focused therapy and integrated CBT/DBT and aspects of mentalization.

THE SUPERVISION HOUR BEGINS

Dr. Shafranske: Why don't we start by talking about what would you like to get out of supervision session today. Is there a particular issue that you think would be useful to look at?

Traci: As far as my caseload—there are no case management issues coming up, but my work with John continues to be a struggle. Dr. Shafranske, if it's OK with you, I'd like to take the time to explore this with you.

Dr. Shafranske: I had a chance to review your videotape [and there is] an awful lot to talk about . . . once again a very challenging session. . . . I agree with you there aren't any clinical management issues. [I had the] opportunity to review your notes; [they are] very detailed [and provided] a good sense of the nature of the challenges and how [your] treatment plans are being enacted. I compliment you on the quality of those notes. Let's turn to the tape. What would be helpful [to] start with?

Discussion: Once the supervisor agreed there were no emergent management issues, the agenda for the session was established in a collaborative manner, focusing on the supervisee's expressed needs. Our view of an agenda is somewhat distinct from its use in CBT-focused supervision. We consider the agenda as a more fluid approach that incorporates flexibility in order to be responsive to training issues spontaneously emerging in the supervisory interaction. In addition to setting the agenda, both the supervisor and supervisee commented on the status of cases in general (i.e., issues relating to case management) and the supervisor took the opportunity to provide brief formative feedback (e.g., about the quality and content of her clinical notes).

Traci: What is most pressing on mind right now [is what happened at the end of the session]. . . . I'm finding that week after week every time he is about to leave or end the session, he proceeds to tell me [he] doesn't understand the purpose of therapy or that it has not been helpful . . . [and that] pulls for me to do something. . . . I explained to him the process of therapy . . . [and] he had some notions . . . I had to dispel them but cannot keep going back to explain.

Dr. Shafranske: So why don't we look together at how you understand that behavior from John—seen [in] other sessions. How do you understand that [his questioning] comes up at the end of the session and he almost leaves you with this sense that this is not helping [and he] questions what is therapy? So, maybe we might think together either from dynamic or CBT perspective. How do you see it?

Discussion: The supervisor decided to focus attention on the knowledge dimension of the competency because knowledge is integral to the performance of the competency, and developing a theoretical and science-informed understanding of client dynamics assists psychotherapists in managing their reactions. Also, knowledge and its application were goals of the rotation and would be included in the final summative evaluation.

Traci: Well, I definitely see it as a projection of his own feelings and perhaps that I cannot help him—I don't feel he has ever been helped by anyone before with regards to the family dynamics . . . and his parents not being available to him emotionally, physically; almost experiencing emotional abuse from siblings. . . . I could understand that he feels or that potentially no one could help him—he's never felt helped before, and I can't help but feel completely ineffective and awful every time I leave the session.

Dr. Shafranske: So it pulls something in you as well . . . John begins to get dysregulated there at the end, but it pulls something in you also as a person and as a therapist.

Traci: Absolutely.

Discussion: The supervisee's associations suggested that attention had to shift to explore her personal reactions rather than maintain focus on her knowledge. A shift is made in part because the supervisor knows from past supervision sessions (and the supervisee's course performance) that she understands the theory and has sufficient knowledge to proceed.

Dr. Shafranske: Would it be useful to talk about that at all?

Traci: Sure, yeah. I think that even though I have been doing therapy for a few years now, I'm still considered somewhat of a novice in the grand scheme of things. . . . I think that there is maybe that pull for doubting my own competence or ability to help . . . that maybe I am doing something wrong; but it's interesting because even as I just thought about that, [I recall] that something he has said before or asked if he is missing something . . . there's a piece to this that maybe is missing, and I guess that's kind of how I feel right now.

Dr. Shafranske: So, you are both having a shared experience of "something is missing" in John's life, and the challenges that he has keeps coming up session after session, day after day, probably, for him. So, if we step back for a moment and think. . . . What [do] we understand about John or clients or patients [who] have some of the [same] psychiatric or psychological challenges that John has. Is [what you observe] consistent with any personality style or disorder?

Discussion: The supervisor shifted focus to knowledge, anticipating that one aspect of helping the supervisee to manage her reactions would be to understand the patient's behaviors in light of his personality functioning. He could have moved directly to the parallel process of countertransference/transference, but chose to proceed first with a knowledge focus. This was intended to enhance her use of her existing knowledge; however, the supervisor may also have been (unconsciously) motivated to down-regulate the emotional arousal of the supervision session by redirecting attention to theory. Viewing the videotape (and previous videotapes) of the patient's intense, provocative reactions and dysregulation affected the supervisor as well as the supervisee. This is one of the many advantages of the use of videotape: The supervisor is brought into a more "experience-near" emotional engagement with the patient, supervisee, and the dynamics of the therapy session.

Traci: Yes, I definitely think ... and I know we talked about it with regard to diagnoses—[the patient] definitely meets criteria for both narcissistic personality disorder and borderline personality disorder—at times [they] can feel juxtaposed and similar ... that has been so confusing ... now that I understand more about dynamic theory and orientation ... and how it is conceptualized and how DBT is conceptualized ... [I have] more compassion for him and his fragmented sense of self ... someone who has those traits falling on that spectrum (borderline personality organization) would pull for my internal chaos. [*Discussion continues regarding diagnosis and case conceptualization.*]

Dr. Shafranske: Yes, patients who have those interpersonal challenges often pull from us [reactions]; it seems like that is how you are feeling.

Traci: I feel like I can't do anything—feeling stuck.

Discussion: The supervisee shifted the focus back to her personal reactions, and in the next section, the supervisor challenges her attribution that she "can't do anything," keeping in mind the transference/countertransference transactions possibly influencing the supervisee's view of her work (and competence).

Dr. Shafranske: Do you think that's true ... that you are not doing anything?

Traci: Well, he keeps coming back, so that demonstrates on a very basic level that perhaps I am doing something for him. ... I have seen progress with regard to his ability to identify and label his emotions and even have more of an ability to communicate with others. But I've been working with him for some time, and it still feels pretty ... at times, it can feel stagnant.

Discussion: The supervisee responded to the supervisor's challenge and engaged in reflection, which brought into focus her realistic appraisal of progress and her feeling of being stuck.

Dr. Shafranske: It is a shared experience . . . [and] that maybe at the end of session he [is] beginning to feel once again [that] he has to leave session and go out in the world and some of these real significant issues he has with managing feelings and interpersonal relationships, that he's going to have to face those challenges outside of the session. I noticed, when we look at the first part of session, it seemed like your interventions were very effective. You were actually facilitating some self-reflection. [Then] there was a moment in the session . . . when he began to kind of ramp up and become . . . dysregulated, and I noticed that you were just quiet and very affirming of him. And he just calmed, and he was actually able to begin to think and reflect. So, when you think about that part of session, maybe we can go back and look at that. Do you think you are being helpful to him, when you look at where he was 8 months ago, a year ago?

Traci: Thank you for pointing out. It's sometimes hard to see when that's the feedback I am getting back from the client. So thank you for that.

Dr. Shafranske: You're welcome. We see the work and that he's better able to self-contain and regulate. . . . But there are points (not in this session but in previous sessions) in which he would stand up and yell . . . very difficult in the room I imagine.

Discussion: The supervisor juxtaposed the patient's gradual development of reflection with moments of dysregulation, encouraging the supervisee to reflect on present and past experiences. As we will see, the supervisee redirects back to her feelings, and the supervisor responds and attempts to normalize the supervisee's experience as a form of empathic support. The supervisee later reflected that her initial reaction to supervisor's attempts to normalize did not fully help because she did not want to have the feelings that were being stirred up.

Traci: I so badly want to help him.

Dr. Shafranske: [He] really stirs up those feelings . . . do you think it's a reasonable response, reasonable experience that a therapist will have? Whether one's an intern, predoc, or practicum student [or] someone who's been practicing for 30 years—do you think it's kind of normative that we would feel something like that?

Traci: Yeah, I guess the piece that's coming up . . . I did not feel that . . . I wish I felt secure enough, maybe in my own skills that it would not rattle me at all, but I guess what you are saying is that we are human before anything.

Dr. Shafranske: Yeah, we don't check our humanity outside . . . and it does pull things in us about our competence and our ability to help John . . . clearly you want to help John.

Discussion: The session continued to explore the supervisee's reactions and the management of moments at the end of sessions when the client is highly activated, critical, and doubting. She reflected that this prompted a feeling of responsibility to solve the problem. The supervisor encouraged further reflection, and the supervisee brought in her knowledge of attachment theory.

Traci: He is anticipating . . . it's always in [his] mind when is this relationship going fall apart . . . when am I going to get fired . . . when is my therapist going to say we have to end . . . it makes me sad to think about.

Dr. Shafranske: What comes up for you as you think of that? Or what are you doing with the sadness in the session with him? Your personal reaction to him?

Traci: I think more than anything I want to help him, to help him process so much of the trauma that he has never had the opportunity to even acknowledge, to help him live a life that he is happy with and proud of. And I guess on a human level, sad that he struggles so much.

Dr. Shafranske: Do you think he has a sense of your caring for him?

Traci: I do.

Dr. Shafranske: That you really do want the best for him.

Traci: I do.

Dr. Shafranske: We talk about theory, and we talk about skills, but it is one of the things you bring your clients and particularly to John. It's clear you care a great deal for clients' welfare, and sometimes he may forget it; there are moments where you might forget it, but I want to give you that feedback. That attitude of really wanting to be helpful, to initiate a healing process, really comes through in all of your work. I'm sure in those moments when he leaves after yelling or after saying that this isn't helpful, and you're not helpful, maybe it's hard to hold onto all the good work you are doing with John.

Discussion: The supervisee's knowledge of attachment theory led her to not only gain perspective on the clinical dynamics, his expectation and experience of losses, but also led to a deepening of her affective experience and empathy. She then redirected the focus to clinical skills and at the end of the session inquired how she might address the client's experiences and dysregulation. The supervisor responded by facilitating a discussion of different theoretical approaches that the supervisee is familiar with and in which she has a measure of competence, such as DBT. She critically examined the impact of expressions of empathy expressed to John and considered the use of techniques drawn from transference-focused psychotherapy.

Following this discussion of interventions related to clinical skills, her tone shifted and she said, "It's still difficult." The supervisor was aware that the supervisee was shifting the focus back to her personal reactions, which indicated the depth of her feelings. He decided to explore more fully her responses while being mindful to not shift into a therapeutic role or engage in a therapeutic process with his supervisee (which would constitute a boundary violation and compromise the alliance and integrity of the supervision).

Dr. Shafranske: What comes to mind right now? What is the most difficult thing for you in working with John?

Traci: I think the primary emotion is sadness for witnessing his experience and how much he has had to go through . . . knowing in the moment . . . [there is] only so much I can do . . . it's going to take a long time.

Dr. Shafranske: I am wondering . . . you have mentioned sadness a couple of times and you [seem] to have a sense that it is pulling from you internally. And this isn't to touch on personal issues because this isn't therapy, but when you are sitting with John, do you think that sadness is getting in the way of being with John or is it bringing you closer to him, in a sense empathically?

Discussion: Here the supervisor reminded the supervisee of the model of responsiveness and reactivity (which they had discussed in previous supervision sessions).

Dr. Shafranske: We also talk about emotional reactivity—we get so aroused—we really aren't able to be empathic, and we can get thrown off of our ability to work with the client. Where would you say you are you in terms of that experience? Do you think you are more responsive or do you think that the intensity of his emotion is leading you to be reactive?

Traci: I think that as I've worked with him, I've become less reactive and more responsive, and what I have realized is that the primary emotion he carries is his anger and [it is his way] to defend against sadness. Once I started responding rather than reacting . . . I was able to actually mirror the underlying sadness, and it significantly improved our relationship and his ability to down regulate throughout the session.

Discussion: There is an ebb and flow in the session to which personal reactions, attitudes (i.e., the supervisee's empathic concern for John and sincere desire to help him), reflection, and consideration of knowledge and technical skills contribute. The supervisee's exploration of her personal reactions led to an important insight about her client's use of anger to in part defend against sadness and loss. Her awareness of her countertransference reactions (personal reactivity) was brought into the service of the treatment. It should be emphasized that the supervisor anchored examination of the supervisee's personal reactions to her conduct of treatment, and he did not engage in a form of exploration akin to psychotherapy. This led to the consideration of interventions the supervisee might have used to manage the patient's often-experienced dysregulation at the end of the session. The supervisor offered some possible interventions drawn from DBT and mentalization, which the supervisee was competent in performing.

With the supervision session nearing its close, the supervisor shifted to consideration of safety, given the patient's volatility and past behavior. The supervisor observed with the supervisee that the patient was a large man and could be quite intimidating (e.g., by yelling) and asked directly how she felt about her safety. She responded that she never felt unsafe or threatened. The supervisor pursued this further, discussing what safety measures the supervisee had put in place. She described some practical procedures she had initiated, including asking her peers in the clinic to keep an ear out for any alerts or significant "raises of volume." The session concluded with giving feedback, eliciting comments from the supervisee, and planning. In subsequent sessions, the supervisee reported increased comfort and expanded her ability to down-regulate and to thoughtfully address her client's dysregulation.

REFLECTION

The excerpts and discussion of this supervision session provided a glimpse of competency-based clinical supervision as practiced. In our view, the effectiveness of this session (and supervision, generally) was determined by the intentional focus on the contributions of the knowledge, skills, and values and attitudes essential to the conduct of the treatment as well as attention to the supervisory alliance (and the other aspects of competency-based clinical supervision). The importance of the development of the contract, initiated at the beginning of supervision, cannot be overstated. This involved articulating the goals of the supervision and setting mutual expectations. It was decided that one of the primary training goals was to enhance the supervisee's competence in conducting psychodynamic psychotherapy. The goals were further refined specific to the clinical needs of the case and included theoretical and clinical integration of CBT and DBT (in which she had developed competence through previous training) and transference-focused therapy. Ongoing discussion of the means to achieve the supervision goals and soliciting feedback about the helpfulness of supervisory interventions with a spirit of openness contributed to the effectiveness of the work and enhanced the alliance.

The session also illustrated the use of the learning cycle, which places emphasis on direct observation (i.e., videotape review), encouragement of supervisee reflective practice, provision of evaluation, and ongoing formative feedback, which leads to planning. Although the discussion in this chapter focused on the supervision process with attention on facilitating the supervisee's self-awareness and clinical competence, the supervisor and supervisee remained mindful of their first obligation: client welfare. This is reflected throughout the session (and course of supervision) in the supervisee's commitment to her client and her supervisor's engagement in facilitating the conditions for effective case oversight and supervision and use of an explicit, metatheoretical, competency-based approach to clinical supervision.

CORE COMPETENCIES AND APPLICATIONS IN SUPERVISION

4

Multiculturalism and Diversity

Supervision of multicultural and diversity competence is an ethical imperative. No matter the nature of the clinical service, individual differences and contextual factors must be considered and incorporated throughout professional practice. Although psychology graduate students receive instruction in sociocultural perspectives, it is in clinical supervision that supervisees develop skill in applying principles and knowledge to ensure culturally sensitive and appropriate psychological services. Crucial to training is the modeling of attitudes (as well as practices) by the supervisor that conveys respect for diversity and commitment to multicultural competence. Falender and Shafranske (2004) defined *supervision diversity* or *multicultural competence* as

> incorporation of self-awareness by both supervisor and supervisee and is an interactive encompassing process of the client or family, supervisee-therapist, and supervisor, using all of their [multiple]

http://dx.doi.org/10.1037/15962-004
Supervision Essentials for the Practice of Competency-Based Supervision, by C. A. Falender and E. P. Shafranske

diversity identities. It entails awareness, knowledge, and appreciation of the intersection among the client's, supervisee-therapist's, and supervisor's assumptions, values, biases, expectations, and worldviews; integration and practice of appropriate, relevant and sensitive assessment and intervention strategies and skills and consideration of the larger milieus of history, society, and sociopolitical variables. (p. 125)

Multicultural competence, or "diversity" as it is described in the American Psychological Association (APA) *Supervision Guidelines* (2014, 2015), explicitly acknowledges both competence (knowledge, skills, and values/attitudes) and attention to multiple diversity identity statuses of supervisor, supervisee, and client. Two guidelines specifically speak to this issue. The second APA supervision guideline states, "Supervisors planfully strive to enhance their diversity competence to establish a respectful supervisory relationship and to facilitate the diversity competence of their supervisees" (APA, 2014, p. 15) and the fourth guideline states, "Supervisors aim to be knowledgeable about the effects of bias, prejudice, and stereotyping. When possible, supervisors model client/patient advocacy and model promoting change in organizations and communities in the best interest of their clients/patients" (APA, 2014, p. 16). It is incumbent on supervisors not simply to be respectful, self-aware, up to date on literature and research but also to infuse multiculturalism and diversity throughout all aspects of clinical and supervision practice.

Psychologists tend to overestimate their multicultural competence (Hansen et al., 2006). Even when psychologists and trainees possess such competence, they may not perform in keeping with the competent treatment (Sehgal et al., 2011). Similarly, in clinical supervision, supervisors profess to discuss and raise multiculturalism with their supervisees; however, supervisees have countered that if any discussion comes up, it is because the supervisee initiates it (Duan & Roehlke, 2001). In group supervision, multicultural conflicts with supervisors and misapplication of multicultural theories, both indicative of a lack of multicultural competence, exacerbate group conflict (Kaduvettoor et al., 2009) and detract from client care. For supervisees, pain and significant worry about client welfare have been inflicted by culturally insensitive supervisors (Jernigan, Green, Helms, Perez-Gualdron, & Henze, 2010; Singh & Chun, 2010) who may misunderstand the client presentation, generally as a result of stereotyping, bias, and lack of multicultural competence.

We believe that the multidimensional ecological comparative approach, a model introduced by Falicov (2014), provides an excellent structural frame for multicultural and diversity discourse and intervention in supervision and clinical practice. For the supervisee and supervisor, the generic ecosystemic parameters include (a) immigration and acculturation, (b) ecological context (c) family organization, and (d) family life cycle of the client in the context of the supervisee and supervisor. That is, from a postmodern position of "not-knowing" and curiosity, the supervisor and supervisee consider each of these factors and the worldviews, biases, and understanding that arise from cultural borderlands or overlapping ecological dimensions. Falicov described ecological niches or multiple contexts that include collective identities of belonging, participation, and identification. *Niches* are shared cultural borderlands, overlapping similar and differing areas, such as race, religion, ethnicity, or gender, among any members of the supervision triad (e.g., client and supervisee). This conceptualization moves the discussion and understanding beyond a simple consideration of ethnicity and provides a means to place culture in the foreground of clinical practice and supervision.

Frequently, we find that supervisees are concerned that they are limited in understanding their clients because of a lack of shared identities. For example, a Chinese American supervisee reported that the mother in his Armenian American family therapy case assumed and often stated that they were sure he had no idea about their culture, and the supervisee was embarrassed because that was true. His supervisor suggested that this presented an opening to explore how the mother and family members viewed divorce, in this case, and what it meant to each of them in a cultural context. Adopting a stance of curiosity and respect opened the door to the family sharing and the supervisee understanding that certain familial aspects (reliance on mother's extended family, respect across generations) were familiar to him, whereas others (privacy and estrangement from the father's family) were not. Generationally, the supervisee was closer in age to the oldest child, and reflected on the loss of socioeconomic status inflicted on the family by the situation. The family took ownership to explain and explore how to navigate the difficult relationship with the father who had left the family, much to the shame of the wife and children, and how to face the community that was privy to many details of the estrangement. The supervisee, in supervision, reflected on some unexpected commonalities between the client and his family of origin, including intense shame and the community response to the separation. The process of conceptualization moved the supervisee beyond cultural stereotypes and overgeneralizations and into a receptive, responsive mode. The supervisor, who was from the parents' generation, modeled knowing and not-knowing stances (Falicov, 2014) addressing specific dynamics observed live between the mother and the children. The mother described herself as overly permissive in general but admitted her permissiveness had become even greater, overindulging the children to make up for what was happening and to assuage her guilt over the divorce. The supervisee was eager to suggest a behavior reward strategy to reduce the overindulgence and enable the children to earn rewards. In this instance, the supervisor urged cultural not-knowing and assisted the supervisee in having the family elaborate on what the newfound permissiveness meant to each of them. This pathway led to the family realization that the abundant gifts may have covered up intense feelings of loss; the gifts were distractions (especially the video game devices) that resulted in distance, avoidance, and isolation of the family members. Supervision, in this case, entailed a combination of knowledge, skills, and attitudes, which helped supervisees reflect on their emotional responses and differentiate their experience from that of the family in therapy.

We suggest attending to multiple multicultural identities from the beginning of the formation of the supervisory alliance. This may take the form of a small, purposeful self-disclosure by the supervisor or a discussion of the importance of considering the worldviews and personal contributions we bring to case assessment, conceptualization, and treatment planning. The disclosure could be, "Being from a different generation from you and the clients, we need to consider the differing worldview we bring." The disclosure is in the service of highlighting even obvious cultural differences—or those that might be inferred incorrectly. Incorrect inferences and the assumptions that follow may strain or rupture the supervisory alliance. For example, a supervisee from Singapore reported that her supervisor, assuming she was Japanese, chastised her for not returning to help "her people" after a tsunami hit Japan. The supervisor committed cultural microaggressions in assuming the country of origin and the values and cultural obligations of the supervisee. Such microaggressions (i.e., behavioral or verbal, unintentional or intentional interactions or exchanges) can denigrate, invalidate, or create hostility while heightening differences related to cultural identities (e.g., ethnicity, race) and have a harmful or discordant impact on the relationship (Sue et al., 2007).

VIGNETTES

In this section, we present two vignettes to illustrate the multiple aspects of diversity that influence identity and interpersonal relations. Consider these multicultural dimensions within the context of supervision.

Vignette 1

In presenting one of her cases to her new supervisor, a 28-year-old White Californian, the supervisee began by saying that the father in the case migrated from South Africa and the mother was from the Midwestern United States. The supervisor interrupted and angrily asked why the supervisee would begin with that information rather than the presenting problem. The supervisee explained that she conceptualized the couple's issue in a cultural frame, as did the couple, who were seeing the world so differently, due in part to being in an interracial marriage. The supervisor reflected that those were assumptions and that they were biasing the supervision and potentially the treatment. The supervisor asked the supervisee to simply present the data and not discuss the clients themselves. The supervisee was upset because she was trying to explain that part of the essential dynamic of the case was that the husband was Black,

an immigrant, and significantly older than his wife. He held highly traditional views of women, and his wife had become increasingly depressed
and isolated and was finding it increasingly difficult to be with him because
he did not want her to go back to school to obtain the graduate degree she
desired, although he had promised her that she could when they married
2 years prior. The supervisee further wanted to explain that, as a Black
woman herself, this was a complex client constellation for her, and she
wanted to address her own feelings about the clients as a means of gaining
greater insight into how to proceed.

If the supervisor came to you for consultation on the supervision,
what would you say? What questions would you ask? Some potential questions to the supervisor might be,

- Are you approaching his particular supervisee and/or case differently
  than you usually do in supervision? If so, why?
- What about the description of the diversity of the clients caused you
  to become angry and to interrupt? What triggered your reaction?
  When you are triggered in supervision, how do you usually address
  it? (Then especially commend the supervisor for coming to you for
  consultation.)
- How do you think the supervisee responded to you? Was that a strain
  or a rupture to your supervisory alliance, or do you have a supervisory
  alliance established? Have you previously discussed your own and the
  supervisee's diversity identities and how these will impact treatment
  and assessment of clients?

Consider your own competence dealing with supervision of the multiple diversity identities in the clients, supervisee, and yourself. Think of
your knowledge, skills, and attitudes and the intersections of these. For
example, if you share cultural borderlands of gender and age with the
supervisee and the supervisee shares borderlands of race with the husband, but there is vast diversity in country of origin, traditional value
systems, beliefs about gender roles, educational levels, and likely multiple
other identities, consider the impact these similarities and differences will
have on your supervision of this particular trainee.

Other questions you might ask to encourage the supervisor to respond to the supervisee could include the following,

- Had the supervisor previously discussed expectations for case description and presentation in supervision?
- Should the supervisor request an immediate meeting with the supervisee to repair the rupture or strain?
- How can the supervisor move forward to ensure that the supervisee is receiving appropriate supervision of the case?
- The supervisor was correct in needing to know more information about the depression of the wife and the presenting problems, but why was it so distressing that the problem was framed in a cultural context?

Vignette 2

The supervisee was an international student from the Philippines. The supervisor was a 55-year-old White male psychologist. The supervisee described his new clients, a Filipino family with two teenage sons who were rebellious and failing in school. The supervisee said that the family wanted him to visit their home because they wanted to pray about the problem and felt that the supervisee had to do this with them to proceed with therapy. Further, the therapist could thereby meet the extended family members, including the 97-year-old great-grandfather, the patriarch of the family who does not go out of the home but is instrumental in every decision made. Further, the family wanted the therapy to be conducted in Tagalog, a language the supervisee/therapist and family shared. The supervisor stated that none of this was possible because it would constitute a multiple relationship and, thus, was ethically untenable. Further, there was no capacity to supervise in Tagalog because there was no supervisor at the agency who spoke that language.

- What are some of the supervisory issues raised in this situation?
- What are the cultural borderlands, worldviews, and competence?
- What are the tensions that arise among institutions, supervisors, supervisees/therapists, and clients and how those could be addressed?

- How could the cultural borderlands be transformed into a strength rather than a liability (Pettifor, Sinclair, & Falender, 2014)?

RESPECT FOR AN INDIVIDUAL'S DIVERSITY: COMPLEX CHALLENGES

An additional diversity issue concerns instances in which a supervisee's (or clinician's) multicultural commitments and loyalties may conflict with client needs or the values of the profession. Religion is rarely discussed in clinical supervision (Inman et al., 2014), nor is it addressed in graduate education and clinical training (Shafranske & Cummings, 2013). Also, religion is significantly less salient to psychologists compared with the general U.S. population; this appears to influence their attitudes and lack of attention to the clinical relevance of client religiousness or spirituality (Shafranske, 2014). Increasingly, values conflicts have resulted in legal action when supervisees decline to work with a particular client because of the supervisee's religious beliefs and values (e.g., *Julea Ward v. Polite*, 2012; *Keeton v. Anderson-Wiley*, 2011; *Ward v. Wilbanks*, 2010). For example, Jennifer Keeton, a student in a master's program in school counseling at a Georgia state school, informed faculty that because her Christian faith viewed "homosexuality" as an immoral lifestyle choice, she advocated that the client change through conversion therapy. When faculty intervened and offered her a remediation plan, she refused, was expelled, and sued the university. The court ruled that Keeton was not required to change her beliefs, but she could not impose them on her clients.

Julea Ward, a student in a master's counseling program at Eastern Michigan University, stated that her Christian faith prohibited her from "affirming homosexuality," which she believed was immoral and a lifestyle choice. When in her second year she was assigned a practicum case in which the client was in a same-sex relationship, she told her supervisor she could see the client for other issues but was not able to treat the issue of the homosexual relationship. After refusing remediation, a process ensued culminating in her expulsion. She brought suit against the school for infringement of her First Amendment rights under the U.S. Constitution, and the lower court deferred to the school for their neutral policies and issued a summary judgment (*Ward v. Wilbanks*, 2010). However, the appeals court concluded that if the facts were viewed in Ms. Ward's favor, a reasonable jury could decide that Ms. Ward—not the university—should prevail. Discounting the summary judgment, the decision stated, "A reasonable jury could conclude that Ward's professors ejected her from the counseling program because of hostility toward her speech and faith, not due to a policy against referrals" (*Julea Ward v. Polite*, 2012). Further, the court concluded that the American Counseling Association (ACA; 2005) Code of Ethics does not prohibit values-based referrals. That is, the court's interpretation was that the ethics code allows appropriate referrals when a therapist "determine[s] an inability to be of professional assistance to clients . . . [and avoids] entering or continuing counseling relationships" (ACA, 2005, p. 6). However, this point has been disputed because there are different responsibilities for a supervisee than for a licensed practitioner; the ACA has since revised its code of ethics to clarify all aspects of this (ACA, 2014).

The appeals court determined whether a university policy, designed and adopted to further a legitimate educational goal, is applied equally to all students regardless of their religion. These cases and the processes highlight the importance of consideration of knowledge, skills, and attitudes, parsing these in competency assessments and reflectively addressing values, conflicts, and attitudes incompatible with the code of ethics or the professional setting.

These decisions inform how faculty, supervisors, and programs should approach situations in which students choose to perform in accordance with their personal values in the professional arena and when these values conflict with standards of professional ethics and behavior. This can be achieved by adding explicit statements such as, "Trainees do not need to give up their personal and/or religious values" (Bieschke & Mintz, 2012, p. 202) and "Trainees are expected to attain both demographic competency and demonstrate the competency of dynamic worldview inclusivity" (Bieschke & Mintz, 2012, p. 202). This wording and concept will be an important addition to the mind-set of programs and supervisors and to the text of all recruitment and program description documents. However, even with this informed consent agreement, supervisees may find that they encounter clients with whom they have a value conflict. Creating an environment of mutual respect (Curry, 2015) and reflection are essential components.

Supervisors of individuals who do not feel competent to work with a client could frame the situation like any difficult one—one's first suicidal client or any number of clients whose life situations, histories, and presentations vary dramatically from the supervisee. It is critical for the supervisor to adopt a reflective, value-neutral stance. The supervisor can then collaboratively (with the supervisee) assess the supervisee's knowledge, skills, and values/attitudes to determine which are strengths and which are in development and may be leading to the supervisee's desire to not work with the client. Most of this work would have already been accomplished in the process of alliance formation; the supervisor can review the foundational work to develop the alliance and frame it in this context as a new opportunity and challenge. It is a supervisory ethical responsibility to delegate client responsibility to a supervisee and "take reasonable steps to authorize only those responsibilities that persons can be expected to perform competently on the basis of their education, training, or experience, either independently or with the level of supervision being provided" (APA, 2010, Standard 2.05(2)). Thus, a supervisor may determine that the client is beyond the supervisee's present competence and may develop a plan for observation of the therapy by a more experienced staff member, conduct cotherapy with the supervisor, or another experienced and competent clinician with an LGBTQ client, supplement these interventions with readings and experiential activities, review using video, and/or take other steps collaboratively defined with the supervisee as part of the learning trajectory.

In our workshops, we have found that individuals role-playing these situations often approach the discussion from the perspective of asking the supervisee to identify the most difficult client situation with which he or she has previously dealt. From there, participants explore strategies and techniques, culminating in a discussion of how they felt as they progressed and as therapeutic successes occurred. Some supervisors may disclose that they had a client whose belief structures differed dramatically from their own and how they were able to develop empathy for the client and work respectfully. A combination of self-awareness regarding attitudes, openness to exploration of emotional response, and consideration of knowledge and skills, all components of competency-based supervision, lead to adherence to dynamic worldview inclusivity.

CONCLUSION

Given the complexity and importance of the task, clinical supervision bears particular responsibility to ensure the development of multicultural competence in the next generation of health service psychologists. Supervisors need to carefully assess their own competence and commitment and be mindful of the impact of the attitudes and skills that they model and the knowledge and skills they use. In addition, supervisors facilitate professional development by encouraging supervisee self-awareness of the multiple cultural identities and perspectives that influence understanding of their clients and the values that animate their work. Finally, clinical supervision supports the implementation of evidence-based practice (APA Presidential Task Force on Evidence-Based Practice, 2006) by ensuring that client values and preferences are taken into consideration along with the extant scientific literature and supervisee and supervisor expertise when providing clinical services.

5

Addressing Personal Factors, Responsiveness, and Reactivity

Providing psychological services, particularly psychotherapy, is an "irreducibly human encounter" (Norcross & Lambert, 2014, p. 402) and, as such, is influenced by personal as well as professional factors. Graduate education and clinical training assists supervisees to incorporate a professional stance and shapes their ways of interacting with clients and other professionals in the clinical setting. Such training builds on the interpersonal qualities and personal background of the clinician. Shafranske and Falender (2008) reflected:

> Each of us, well before we ever entered graduate school or met our first client, formed fundamental ways of relating to others. We assimilated family and culture-bound styles of interpersonal relating, internalized attitudes and beliefs about human nature, and absorbed the worldviews and mores of the ethnic, social, political, cultural, intellectual, gendered, economic, and spiritual communities in which we

http://dx.doi.org/10.1037/15962-005
Supervision Essentials for the Practice of Competency-Based Supervision, by C. A. Falender and E. P. Shafranske

inhabited. These inescapable frameworks of identity, forged out of interaction with the surround, establish fundamental assumptions about self and others, ethical values, and instill a feeling-sense of being at home in the world. Not solely products of internalization, our personal identities reflect dynamic, emergent sources of meaning and motivation . . . we may question (and even reject) the original constituents of our multicultural identities; however, the imprint of these seminal influences remains. (p. 98)

Consistent with appreciation for the influences of multicultural identity, a host of personal factors form inescapable frameworks of meaning that influence relationships, including professional relationships with patients. Clinical supervision provides a relationship, context, and process to develop greater awareness of the role of personal factors affecting professional practice and to safeguard the client from inappropriate behavior emanating from such influences. In this chapter, we take up the ethical requirement to address personal factors, discuss the nature of personal reactivity (commonly referred to in the literature as *countertransference*), and present a supervision approach to explore and manage personal factors. For a supervisory example on handling supervisee reactivity, see Chapter 3.

ORIENTING THE SUPERVISEE TO PERSONAL FACTORS IN CLINICAL SUPERVISION

The initial orientation to personal factors occurs at the beginning of supervision when discussing expectations in the context of the supervision contract. It is important to frame awareness of "personal contribution to therapy and supervision" as a competency benchmark (Fouad et al., 2009, p. S22), an ethical requirement (American Psychological Association [APA; 2010] *Ethical Principles of Psychologists and Code of Conduct*, Standard 2.06), and a necessary component of clinical supervision, in accordance with the *Guidelines for Clinical Supervision in Health Service Psychology* (APA, 2015). Further, informed consent should be obtained, consistent with Standard 7.04,

Student Disclosure of Personal Information. Psychologists do not require students or supervisees to disclose personal information in course- or program-related activities, either orally or in writing, regarding sexual history, history of abuse and neglect, psychological treatment, and relationships with parents, peers, and spouses or significant others except if (1) the program or training facility has clearly identified this requirement in its admissions and program materials or (2) the information is necessary to evaluate or obtain assistance for students whose personal problems could reasonably be judged to be preventing them from performing their training- or professionally related activities in a competent manner or posing a threat to the students or others. (APA, 2010, p. 12)

Like other competencies, a unique set of knowledge, skills, and attitudes are used in its performance.

Knowledge

There are significant differences in knowledge about personal factors (or countertransference) between supervisees, depending on the nature of their education and previous clinical training. For example, those trained in graduate programs with a psychoanalytic orientation have likely received a great deal of exposure to theories of countertransference and may be well versed in examining their personal contributions to the therapeutic process. However, those whose education and training was focused on cognitive or behavioral models may have a lesser understanding of such concepts. Therefore, again in keeping with our approach, supervisors should assess the supervisee's knowledge rather than make assumptions.

Whereas personal factors have been traditionally understood through the conceptual lens of countertransference (derived from psychoanalytic theory), we have proposed and advocate for an atheoretical and phenomenological approach.[1] In our view, a host of personal factors, including multicultural identities and values, (as well as unresolved personal conflicts; see

---

[1] This chapter draws from material published in Falender and Shafranske (2004, 2012a) and Shafranske and Falender (2008).

Hayes & Gelso, 2001, for further discussion) contribute to the fundamental ways in which we understand and relate to ourselves and others. This perspective is not intended to diminish the importance of conflict but rather to furnish an enlarged view that takes into consideration all the personal contributions that influence therapeutic and supervisory relationships. Further, we argue that all clinical understanding and conduct is, by definition, influenced by professional and personal factors (including personal and culture-based values); therefore, gaining awareness of the perspectival nature of understanding and relating is an important competency to develop.

The influence of personal factors, which affect clinicians at all times, has a particular impact on the therapeutic process when clients are in heightened states of emotion—for instance, when they are uncovering and dealing with circumstances of loss, trauma, guilt, or interpersonal conflict. A measure of emotional arousal in the supervisee is normative and, in fact, is required to make psychological contact with the client, no matter what the psychological issues or health conditions they are dealing with in treatment. It is the clinician's ability to be emotionally engaged that facilitates understanding and contributes to the client's sense of being understood. However, there are clinical situations that arouse heightened emotional reactivity in the clinician and which negatively affect his or her ability to be attuned to the client's experience and to respond empathically.

We envision a continuum of emotional responsiveness to emotional reactivity. On one end of the continuum, there is emotional arousal that leads to responsiveness and results in empathy, and on the other end there is overarousal (or at times a "deadening" lack of arousal) that provokes reactivity and forecloses empathy with the client's subjective experience. Such emotional reactivity (which may be seen as the sine qua non of countertransference) limits attunement, potentially resulting in the loss of psychological contact with the patient and (depending on the nature of the reactivity) imperiling the therapeutic relationship. This depiction refers to reactivity in the extreme; however, there are far more subtle instances of reactivity that influence the therapeutic relationship and process. Reactions may be generated by differences in attitudes and beliefs, personal and cultural biases, and worldviews, or by experiences held in common with the patient or triggered by vicarious exposure to trauma. Supervisors assist the supervisee by providing perspective on the role of personal factors and developing skill in recognizing the contributions of personal factors as well as managing both subtle and dramatic manifestations of reactivity.

Skills

Skills in self-awareness and reflectivity are required to recognize the influence of personal factors and manage reactivity. Supervision supports the development of these skills by engaging the supervisee in self-reflective practice and by modeling awareness and attention to manifestations of reactivity. Kiesler (2001) provided an approach to identify reactivity in his operational definition of *countertransference*: "distinctly different, unusual or idiosyncratic acts or patterns of therapist experience and/or actions toward a client [that constitute] deviations in baselines" in the clinician's (or supervisee's or supervisor's) usual practice (pp. 1061–1062). Commitment to reflective practice requires practice and encouragement of the supervisor. Perhaps the most important assistance the supervisor contributes to the supervisee's development is to bring empathic interest to the supervisee's personal impact on the therapeutic process, to reinforce the supervisee's developing self-awareness, to avoid inducing shame, and to maintain the clear boundary between supervision and psychotherapy.

Attitudes

As with most competencies, the development of awareness of the influence of personal factors and managing reactivity rests on the personal and professional attitudes of the supervisee. Supervisees who manifest curiosity and self-awareness genuinely value self-knowledge, are committed to patient welfare, and are well prepared to engage in reflective practice. In addition to personal attitudes, professional attitudes and dispositions embedded in different theoretical orientations should be respectfully considered, drawing attention to the empirical literature on common factors and the factors that influence alliance and effective therapeutic relationships. Professionalism and commitment to APA ethics and benchmark competencies inform attitudes encouraging reflective practice across all theoretical lines.

THE SUPERVISORY PROCESS

Supervision bears responsibility for client welfare as well as for the development of competence in the supervisee. Gaining awareness of the personal factors that influence the process and outcome of psychological treatment serves both interests. The supervisor initiates work in this area by identifying the awareness of personal contributions to be a competence under development and setting expectations for examination of this aspect of professional practice. It is important to keep in mind and to explicitly remind the supervisee that exploration of personal factors or reactivity is not psychotherapy, nor does supervision provide a setting to work through personal conflicts—the boundary between supervision and psychotherapy is distinct. An orientation and preparation to the supervision of personal factors and reactivity is accomplished by attention to the following:

- *Alliance.* The alliance has been found to play an integral role in both comfort and likelihood of disclosure of personal reactivity (or countertransference) in supervision (Pakdaman, Shafranske, & Falender, 2015). Therefore, close attention should be placed on the establishment of a collaborative working relationship and alliance before initiating exploration of personal factors.
- *Supervisory contract.* The expectation that personal factors will be a component of the supervision is mutually discussed in developing the supervisory contract, including developing self-awareness, engaging in reflective practice, using supervision effectively, and managing personal reactions. These are explicitly identified as professional competencies.
- *Explicit orientation to personal factors.* The supervisor introduces the conceptual framework for understanding the role of personal factors in the conduct of psychotherapy and other professional activities. Empha-

sis is placed on the normative nature of the confluence of personal and professional factors in psychological practice. Disclosure by the supervisor of examples in which personal factors affected their professional work, including how they managed such reactions, encourages openness to this dimension of practice for the supervisee.

- *Personal factors in supervision and parallel process.* The supervisor affirms that personal factors influence supervisory as well as therapeutic relationships and provides examples of how such factors (e.g., interpersonal style or individual differences)—that is, multicultural factors—may affect supervision. Further, the supervisor should describe the nature of parallel process and provide examples of how supervisors and supervisees can address such clinical dynamics in supervision.

- *Modeling.* The supervisor models appropriate disclosure in briefly sharing how his or her personal factors, including multicultural identities, contribute to clinical practice and supervision.

Following this introduction, the supervisor encourages the supervisee to reflect on his or her personal reactions—to "reflect-on-action"—and to consider how personal factors are influencing engagement with the patient. Joint review of video material is an important vehicle for identifying and exploring personal factors. Emphasis is placed on the identification of idiosyncratic states of mind and behaviors, as discussed earlier (Kiesler, 2001). Supervision procedures such as interpersonal process recall (Kagan & Kagan, 1997) provide a systematic approach to exploring personal reactivity. Mindfulness training may also be useful in creating the conditions to identify and process personal reactions (Safran, Muran, Stevens, & Rothman, 2008).

ADDRESSING REACTIVITY

Close attention by the supervisor is required when emotional reactivity affects the therapeutic relationship. In such situations, the supervisor must carefully balance responsibilities to ensure patient welfare by, for example, providing an effective therapeutic relationship and enhancing supervisee competence. Effective countertransference management draws on both personal and professional competencies, including self-insight, self-integration, ability to experience and manage anxiety, empathy, and conceptualization skills (Gelso & Hayes, 2002). The following stages reflect the emergence of reactivity and recommended supervisor interventions and processes to manage reactivity and enhance supervisee self-awareness and competence.

State 1. Responsiveness and Engagement

Responsiveness and *engagement* refer to therapeutic conditions in which the supervisee is maintaining psychological contact with the patient and empathically and appropriately responding, facilitating the therapeutic process. Although personal factors inevitably influence the supervisee and the treatment process, these factors are generally out of awareness and in the background. The supervisor engages the supervisee in exploration of personal factors that may be contributing to treatment and normalizes the probable impact.

State 2. Reactivity

In this state, the supervisee is emotionally reacting rather than empathically responding to the patient. Again, such clinical situations range from the subtle to the dramatic, with corresponding impact on the patient and varying degrees of awareness in the supervisee. Not surprisingly, reactivity can be activated by clinical emergencies, exposure to trauma, and the challenges faced when working with highly vulnerable patients presenting with complex, persistent, and severe psychiatric or personality disorders (see Chapter 3 for an illustration).

State 3. Identifying the Marker and Becoming Reflective

This state is initiated by the development of awareness of the supervisee's idiosyncratic states of mind or behaviors, indicating that something unusual (i.e., out of the ordinary) is going on. The supervisor encourages self-reflectivity in the supervisee and points out indicators of reactivity as evidenced by video review or self-report. Developing skill in the identification of subtle shifts in state of mind and attention to deviations of clinical behavior is an important component of clinical competence. The supervisor should note and reinforce the supervisee's openness to examine their personal reactions and behaviors (attitude), developing ability to recognize the influence of personal factors and instances of reactivity (skill), and their application of the model (knowledge). During the exploration of the personal factors and experiences leading to reactivity, it is critical that the supervisor maintains a clear boundary between supervision and therapy. It is in heightened states of supervisee reactivity that the supervisor may be inclined (on the basis of his or her own reactivity and the influence of the supervisee) to engage errantly in a process resembling a therapeutic interaction. One safeguard is to consistently redirect attention to how past experiences of supervisees and their subsequent emotional reactivity is influencing their being with their patient (see Chapter 3 for an illustration). In heightened states of reactivity, the supervisee may subtly influence the supervisor to shift from a supervisory to a therapeutic role, which would be unethical and constitute a boundary violation. Again, the supervisor should redirect to the supervisee's ability to engage the patient in clinical work, keeping the focus on the supervisee's work and relationship with the client. During this stage, it is useful to draw on the intellectual resources and knowledge of clinical theory to provide a context for learning from the experience, as well as to gain a sense of control. The supervisor has to balance normalizing the supervisee's experience with stressing the importance of keeping the patient's welfare as the priority by better managing reactivity. Supervisors have to be mindful of addressing these issues with sensitivity (and particularly not induce shame) and professionalism as a supervisor (and not as a therapist). Depending on the nature, extent, and impact of the reactivity, the supervisor may consider recommending to the supervisee consultation with a clinician (not the supervisor nor a member of the clinical faculty) to address the personal reactivity and its impact on the supervisee's professional performance.

State 4. Planning

The last state, planning, draws on what has been learned through the process of identifying the marker of reactivity and exploring the contextual, relational, and personal factors (including client factors) that contributed to the supervisee's reactivity. Supervisor and supervisee discuss what steps or interventions, if any, should be initiated to enhance the alliance and to ensure the progress of treatment. Also, the supervisor should engage in a discussion of the supervisory experience and normalize and address any discomfort the supervisee may experience. The supervisor should reinforce the supervisee's professional attitude and openness, application of knowledge, and development of reflective skills as components of competence as the supervisee reestablishes emotional responsiveness with the patient. The following points inform the approach and discussion:

■ The supervisory alliance must be established before reactivity can be meaningfully addressed and managed.

■ Understanding the nature and influence of personal factors, including reactivity, is a clinical competency and is required in the process of clinical supervision.

■ Reactivity (or countertransference) is an informer of the therapeutic process and can provide important insight into the client's relational world, the therapist's relational world, and the schemas or internal object relations affecting the clinical relationship. Both objective and subjective forms of countertransference may occur in the therapeutic process, and require differentiation.

■ Instances of reactivity may involve positive and/or negative emotional responses in the supervisee and take the forms of distinctly different, unusual, or idiosyncratic acts or patterns of therapist experience and/or actions toward the patient and include parallel processes involving the supervisory relationship.

■ It is critical to maintain the boundary between supervision and psychotherapy when addressing personal reactivity or the influence of personal factors. Any exploration of supervisee personal factors must be specifically related to the conduct of the treatment provided by the supervisee.

- How supervisees address and manage personal reactions is more important than the fact they occur.
- Clinical competence includes the awareness of personal factors that influence the therapeutic process as well as skills in effectively bringing countertransference reactions into the service of the treatment.

SUMMARY

Clinical supervision provides a relational context and process for understanding the role of personal factors in professional practice and learning to manage personal reactivity. Knowledge of a transtheoretical approach to personal factors (as presented in this chapter and by Kiesler, 2001), skills in identifying and reflecting on reactivity and idiosyncratic states of mind and behavior, and attitudes of openness to exploration of personal contributions to professional practice each contribute to the development of this competency.

6

Ensuring Legal, Ethical, and Regulatory Competence

Ethical, legal, and regulatory issues may not necessarily be covered systematically in clinical supervision. Nevertheless, an essential component of competency-based supervision is identifying and monitoring knowledge, skills, and attitudes regarding legal, ethical, and regulatory issues as they arise in all clinical work and determining competence in those. According to the American Psychological Association (APA) *Guidelines for Clinical Supervision in Health Service Psychology* (APA, 2014, 2015), the following are specific competencies:

1. Supervisors model ethical practice and decision-making and conduct themselves in accord with the APA ethical guidelines, guidelines of any other applicable professional organizations, and relevant federal, state, provincial, and other jurisdictional laws and regulations. . . .

http://dx.doi.org/10.1037/15962-006
Supervision Essentials for the Practice of Competency-Based Supervision, by C. A. Falender and E. P. Shafranske

2. Supervisors uphold their primary ethical and legal obligation to protect the welfare of the client/patient. . . .
3. Supervisors serve as gatekeepers to the profession. Gatekeeping entails assessing supervisees' suitability to enter and remain in the field. . . .
4. Supervisors provide clear information about the expectations for and parameters of supervision to supervisees preferably in the form of a written supervisory contract. . . .
5. Supervisors maintain accurate and timely documentation of supervisee performance related to expectations for competency and professional development. (pp. 23–25)

ETHICS

It is important to assess the supervisee's skill at ethical decision making at the beginning of supervision. Graduate students in psychology typically have had only one ethics course, and it may have had a rule-bound, risk management, liability awareness focus. Exposure to positive ethics may be lacking. *Positive ethics* entails aspiring to moral excellence, encouraging psychologists to integrate personal ideals into one's professional life (Knapp & VandeCreek, 2006). A supervisory responsibility is to consider dilemmas from an ethical perspective, use ethical decision making, and model a reflective positive ethics stance. Disciplinary codes represent a minimal standard for practice, and deviation from those may result in misconduct. As Beauchamp and Childress (2009) pointed out, professionals may believe they satisfy moral requirements by fulfilling the letter of the code of ethics, but codes have little emphasis on moral principles such as veracity, justice, and respect for autonomy. These may be reflected in aspirational parts of the code, but not in the enforceable sections.

Gottlieb, Handelsman, and Knapp (2008) provided guidance on how an ethics acculturation model could assist supervisors to inculcate a positive ethics frame for supervisees. They described two processes: (a) maintenance or retention of the ethics and values traditions of the culture of origin and (b) contact and participation or the degree to which students adopt the values, norms, and traditions of the professional culture. The first quadrant is integrational: supervisees integrate their culture of origin with professional values and ethics. The second quadrant is separation: supervisees may make personal decisions and take actions on the basis of their personal value systems without significant integration of professional ethics or values. An example might be the assumption that boundaries associated with friendship are equally applicable in relationships with clients.

Assimilation is the third quadrant in which the professional ethics code is adopted without reference to personal values, potentially leading to simplistic and literal adherence to ethics codes. An example of this might occur when a supervisee abruptly refuses a gift from a client, without regard for professionalism or relationship and cultural factors, by simply telling the client it is against the rules. Marginalization is the fourth quadrant and is marked by low identification with both professional and personal ethical cultures. This is the least desirable outcome and occurs least frequently. An example would be a supervisee who sees a client without supervision for personal financial gain and without regard for the consequences to the client. Integration is the most desirable outcome, as mentioned earlier. For example, when a client gives the supervisee a gift, the supervisee might reflect on the generosity and thoughtfulness of the client, the meaningfulness of the gift, and the significance to the client–supervisee relationship and their work together and then gently describe the dilemma—that the rules prohibit accepting such a gift and that it is essential for the supervisee to adhere to these rules while still honoring the significance and meaning of the gift. Further examples are provided by Knapp, Gottlieb, and Handelsman (2015).

The *Universal Declaration of Ethical Principles for Psychologists* (International Union of Psychological Science [IUPS], 2008) provides an international moral framework developed to inspire psychologists to attain their highest ethical ideals in their professional and scientific work and defines principles based on shared human values. In the global community, it is an important document to understand. The Universal Declaration calls for knowledge of the social and cultural context and adequate self-knowledge of how one's values, experiences, culture, and social context might influence one's actions and interpretations, choices, and recommendations

(Principle II, IUPS, 2008). This code highlights the significance of values and morality in ethical decision making. In the next section, we present some vignettes, and we encourage you to conceptualize the ethical considerations against the backdrop of these models.

Jon went to graduate school after traveling the world for several years after college. He described himself as "highly privileged" and considered graduate school in psychology the ideal way to give back for the advantages and privilege he enjoyed. His first practicum placement in the postmaster's program was working with homeless individuals in a temporary shelter. Jon's client was a 52-year-old male who had had a family and had been a teacher for many years. It was unclear whether his substance abuse induced a psychotic episode or the reverse, but he was only recently sober and was making good progress toward obtaining subsidized housing. He had lost his family and everything he owned. He had always had an interest in photography, a theme that was frequently discussed in therapy because Jon too was a photography buff. In supervision, after about four months of therapy, Jon said that he needed the supervisor's input on which course to follow. It was close to Christmas, and Jon wanted to give his client a camera from his extensive collection of Leicas. His question was whether he should simply give the client the camera as a gift or whether he should pretend it came from a "Make-a-Wish" type of organization.

How would you approach this in supervision? Consider the supervisory alliance, supervision contract, ethical and legal aspects, risk factors, Jon's integration of professional and personal ethics, multiple relationships, diversity, and worldviews that differentiated Jon from the client and how these may have affected Jon's behavior. Consider also the question Jon was asking—not whether to give the camera, but how to give it. And consider using another general ethical decision-making model, one by Koocher and Keith-Spiegel (2008, p. 21–23) that suggests supervisors

- determine that the matter is an ethical one;
- consult available ethical guidelines that might apply to provide a possible mechanism for resolution;
- consider all sources that might influence the kind of decision you will make;

- locate and consult with a trusted colleague;
- evaluate the rights, responsibilities, and vulnerability of all affected parties;
- generate alternative decisions;
- enumerate the consequences of making each decision;
- make the decision; and
- implement the decision.

We encourage including two additional questions. What is the supervisee's and supervisor's emotional response to the dilemma? In this instance, a supervisor might be highly reactive, concerned about the ethical and legal aspects of the dilemmas. And what are the cultural and contextual considerations raised? The diversity in age (generation) and socioeconomic status has to be considered. After determining that there is a significant ethical aspect to this dilemma, what guidelines could be consulted? Consider the guidelines and practices at the site (homeless shelter) at which the therapy is occurring and the *Ethical Principles of Psychologists and Code of Conduct* (APA, 2010). Relevant principles include (a) Beneficence and Nonmaleficence—doing no harm and safeguarding the rights and welfare of those with whom we interact professionally; (b) Fidelity and Responsibility—establishing relationships of trust and awareness of professional responsibilities to society and managing conflicts of interest that could lead to exploitation or harm; (c) Integrity—not engaging in internal misrepresentation of fact nor in subterfuge; and (d) Justice—exercising reasonable judgment and taking precautions to ensure potential biases do not lead to or condone unjust practices (APA, 2010).

Identify specifics from the Code of Conduct (APA, 2010) that apply as well, such as Standard 3.05 Multiple Relationships:

> The psychologist refrains from entering into a multiple relationship if the multiple relationship could reasonably be expected to impair the psychologist's objectivity, competence, or effectiveness in performing his or her functions as a psychologist, or otherwise risks exploitation or harm to the person with whom the professional relationship exists.

Or Standard 3.06 Conflict of Interest. Could Standard 2.01 Boundaries of Competence be a factor? If the supervisee is a novice therapist and focuses on their mutual photography interest, he may not be practicing (even under supervision) within a reasonable boundary. Also consider Standard 2.04 Bases for Scientific and Professional Judgments, whether the supervisee's work has an established professional basis.

What is the worst-case scenario? What could happen if the supervisee gave the client the Leica camera? There is a multitude of personal, legal, and ethical implications. What would the consequence be if the supervisor told Jon he could not give the client the camera? Consider the supervisory relationship, the supervisee's personal factors, the diversity and multicultural factors, and any other aspects that might be relevant, and balance these with the possible benefits that could accrue from giving the client the camera, directly or through an intermediary. The context, diversity factors, and your emotional reaction, as well as that of the supervisee, must all be taken into account. How would you advise the supervisor to proceed using the competency-based model?

MULTIPLE RELATIONSHIPS

In clinical supervision, some multiple relationships may be normative. For example, in internships, supervisors may collaborate with their supervisees on research projects, journal articles, or other projects. In graduate school, a supervisor may be a dissertation chair or a professor in a required seminar. It is wise to consider the broad range of implications and possible repercussions for multiple relationships between supervisors and supervisees.

Gottlieb, Robinson, and Younggren (2007) provided an ethical decision-making model for when a supervisor should engage in multiple relationships with a supervisee. Consider the following questions (adapted from Gottlieb et al., 2007, pp. 245–246):

- Is entering into a relationship in addition to the supervisory one necessary, or should the supervisor avoid it?
- Can the additional relationship potentially cause harm to the supervisee?

- Are there cultural factors to consider?
- If harm seems unlikely or avoidable, would the additional relationship prove beneficial?
- Is there a risk that the additional relationship could disrupt the supervisory relationship?
- Can the supervisor evaluate the matter objectively?

Consider several scenarios:

- An internship director in a small community has been a long-term member of a recovery self-help group. A new internship group started several weeks ago, and to his chagrin, one of the new interns arrived to participate in the self-help group.
- An intern moved with her partner across the country for her internship. In the second month, she disclosed that her partner had a house cleaning service. It was difficult to get customers in the new setting, and her husband needed a few people to use it to get favorable ratings to get him started. She offered the supervisor three free house cleanings by her husband, with the expectation that the supervisor would write a favorable review on Yelp.
- The head of practicum placement at a large city hospital just learned from his students that the supervisor's preschool-age son is in a class taught by the spouse of one of his practicum students.

Consider creative ways to approach these situations, respecting client welfare, the supervisee, and ethical standards.

LEGAL AND ETHICAL CONSIDERATIONS REGARDING SUICIDE RISK

Supervisees encounter many high-risk clients. It is incumbent on the supervisor to know the frequency of these in the setting and to assess the supervisee's readiness to address these situations. Ninety-seven percent of clinicians fear losing a client to suicide (Pope & Tabachnick, 1993), and it is estimated that one in four psychologists will lose a client to suicide during their career (Kleespies & Dettmer, 2000). An estimated 40% of supervisees have had a patient commit suicide or make a serious attempt (Kleespies, 1993); 97% reported that they had at least one client with suicidal ideation or behavior during their training, and 17% had a client commit suicide during training. Moreover, we have observed that supervisees may be unprepared to assess or intervene without training in their practicum, internship, and/or postdoctoral positions because the specifics of handling behavioral emergencies may not have been adequately addressed for each population (e.g., child, young adult, older adults, veterans) in graduate school and definitely not in the sequelae of the suicide. Supervisors have to discuss specific risk factors for the population being served, as well as assessment tools and specific plans to contact the supervisor immediately. Supervisors have to also assist supervisees to deal with the aftermath and follow-up.

Predictably, supervisees who experience a client suicide or attempt, experience feelings of shock, disbelief, failure, sadness, self-blame, guilt, shame, and depression and the possibility of longer-term anxiety and helplessness (Spiegelman & Werth, 2004). The stress of a suicidal client may be even greater for the supervisee than for the supervisor who holds the liability. In their article, "Don't Forget About Me," Spiegelman and Werth (2004) described how as trainees their reactions to a client suicide and attempt were neglected or totally disregarded. Kleespies (1993) identified several reasons for the omission of suicide in training: Supervisees may be at the frontline assessing and treating suicidal clients because faculty often retreat into their own research areas, acknowledgement of the existence of suicidal clients may hinder supervisee morale and recruitment, having experienced a client suicide may be viewed as a failure that supervisors do not want to publicize, or superstitious behavior may lead to thinking that if the phenomenon is not addressed, it will not happen.

Kleespies (1993) proposed a series of procedures addressing assessment, intervention, and resynthesis to better prepare supervisees for the eventuality of suicidal clients. Kleespies found that the intense emotional impact immediately following a client suicide might last from a week to a month. Support and acceptance of the reality, coupled with knowing the supervisee is not alone are indicated. Meeting with and receiving support from the supervisor is essential. The possibility of meeting with other staff who knew the client or had worked with him or her may also be important. Talking with other professionals who had experienced client suicide was reported to be helpful at a later point (but contraindicated immediately). It is important for supervisees to know that they are not alone in the experience and to be helped to deal with the shock they have experienced. Stress management, inoculation, and affect regulation are important client skills (and we believe therapist skills as well) to assist "learned resourcefulness" (Meichenbaum, 2007, p. 513).

Supervisees' emotional needs may not be met following behavioral emergencies and, most particularly, client suicide (Knox, Burkard, Jackson, Schaack, & Hess, 2006). It is most frequently supervisors who inform supervisees of suicides, and the process can be respectful, but some supervisees have reported a perceived lack of support, impersonal debriefing, or a search for causes that seemed to attach blame to the supervisee. Aberrant and unhelpful supervisor responses included informing a supervisee of the suicide in the mailroom, leaving a message for a supervisee on his or her voice mail, jumping to attend immediately to legal ramifications, or generally being unresponsive. Such interventions may cause supervisees to personalize clients' actions because supervisees are less equipped to separate "personal failure from the limitations of the therapeutic process" (Foster & McAdams, 1999, p. 24). Thus, a supervisory challenge is to understand the immediate need for support and the steps that follow to ensure a continuation of the existing supportive supervisory relationship. Personal self-care and monitoring are strongly advocated when suggested in a supportive manner. The process of effective supervision in high-intensity situations is an excellent example of the intersection of knowledge, skills, and attitudes and how the effective supervisor integrates these into the assessment of the supervisee's competence and planning for effective supervision.

ISSUES WITH VIOLENT CLIENTS

Supervisees and early career psychologists are at risk of experiencing violent client behavior perhaps because they are less alert to escalating cues of violence and have less knowledge of how to de-escalate these situations (Guy, Brown, & Poelstra, 1992). Other high-risk situations that supervisors must competently address are sexual harassment by the client and potential for the client to commit violence (Pabian, Welfel, & Beebe, 2009).

Pabian et al. (2009) found that more than three quarters of psychologists queried in a large study were misinformed about their state laws regarding duty to warn, even though most were confident they understood these laws. It is particularly important for supervisors and practitioners to uphold the requirement of legal competence. Pabian et al. found no correspondence between continuing education in legal and ethical issues, graduate education, or experience with violent clients and competence with duty to warn. Practitioners and supervisors have to abide by 2.03 Maintaining Competence (APA, 2010). Also, supervisors have to be particularly attuned to high-risk clients to ensure supervisees have the skill to de-escalate or identify risk behavior early and to seek supervision. Ensuring safety is a critical component of clinical supervision. Pope, Sonne, and Greene (2006) addressed topics therapists do not talk about—including some of the ones just mentioned—and reflected on exploration and creating safety. Such discussions and scenarios are invaluable training devices for enhancing readiness for dealing with high-risk behavior. Assessing the ability to identify escalating or dangerous behaviors (and the skills to manage these) and attitudes (e.g., fear, submission) regarding clients who are potentially dangerous are essential aspects of supervision.

LEGAL AND ETHICAL ISSUES IN THE INTERNET ERA

The impact of the Internet on supervision practice is enormous and multi-faceted. How prepared are supervisors or institutions of learning or training for the resultant culture change? Because technology has enabled distance supervision and a total shift in mind-set, supervisees in the sharing generation share personal information as well as possessions, a Skype account is more important than a driver's license, and virtual communication is equal or even preferable to meeting face-to-face (Beloit College, 2016). One's digital footprint is one's identity, and as supervisees adopt a professional persona, professionalism is essential to the progression. Increasingly, supervisees are ensuring that information on their various websites is reflective of their emerging identity as a psychologist (Asay & Lal, 2014). Specific changes include expressing discomfort when clients contact supervisees via a social network (90.8%), changing privacy settings (89.7%), changing content of social networking sites (74%), and modifying pictures posted since beginning graduate school (61%). The majority felt that social networking and communication were seriously neglected in discussions at training sites.

Discussions and supervisor competence are especially important given the generational divide: Supervisees are more likely to be digital natives and highly familiar and skilled in social media, Internet searches, and general applications, whereas supervisors may lag behind in attitudes, skills, and knowledge in these areas. The Internet is being used for education of clients and promotional activities and as a vehicle for therapeutic modalities, social networking (DeJong et al., 2012), and searches for client and supervisor information (Asay & Lal, 2014).

Medical educators have raised significant concerns about professionalism. Ponce et al. (2013) found that 86% of the Facebook pages of orthopedic surgery resident applicants had no privacy settings, and 16% of the postings contained unprofessional material. A Swedish study of physicians' and medical students' tweets revealed a low rate of unprofessionalism clustered within a small subset of the 237 accounts studied (Brynolf et al., 2013). Gabbard, Kassaw, and Perez-Garcia (2011) observed alcohol, drug, or unprofessional content, language, or patient privacy violations on social network pages, with the majority of medical students blogging under their own name and casting clients or the medical profession in a negative light. They also cautioned about dating websites, where abundant personal information about supervisees, clients, and supervisors could be accessed.

Gabbard et al. (2011) urged supervisors to encourage supervisees to see social media as a mirror and to determine what reflections we want the public (our clients) to see, transforming harm reduction into mental health promotion, embracing the power of social media, and communicating professionalism (expanded from Greysen, Kind, & Chretien, 2010). Some suggestions included pausing before posting to engage in professional reflection, considering the message that one is sending about the individual and the profession, and considering the intent of an Internet search and application of findings (Farnan et al., 2013). An important supervisory strategy is to draw on the competence of the supervisees in social media and on the Internet to discuss the professionalism and ethical aspects of such use. Such discussions may include introducing an ethical problem-solving framework adapted from Clinton, Silverman, and Brendel (2010, pp. 105–107) to assist in decision making about Internet behavior, which entails asking the following questions before using the Internet in client contact or searches:

- Why do I want to conduct this search (the motivation or rationale)?
- Would my search advance or compromise treatment? Would it harm my client or our relationship? Or would it potentially benefit the client?
- Should I obtain informed consent from the client? If not, why not?
- Should I share the results of the search with the client? How will I use the information? How will I deal with undisclosed duty to warn if it arises?
- Should I document the findings of the search in the clinical/medical record?
- How do I monitor my motivations and the ongoing risk or benefit profile regarding searching?

Discussion of social media, social networking, and Internet use provides an excellent opportunity for collaborative discussion because supervisees may be substantially more fluent and competent in Internet use and communication than many supervisors, revealing a generational divide. A respectful process is essential to ensure a thoughtful and appropriate response. Some of the issues rapidly emerging are use of texting with adolescent clients; conducting distance video sessions using emerging technologies; using distance supervision; using Google to search for information regarding clients or applicants to graduate programs, internships, or jobs; "friending" adolescent or young adult clients through a professional social network page; communicating with clients via social networks; or posting pictures that are less than professional and being identified through tags. In medical settings, there is concern that professionals are inadequately attentive to professional vulnerability online and do not take care to restrict access to posted material and to apply the principles of professionalism to online postings and presence (Osman, Wardle, & Caesar, 2012). However, different constituents view postings and appropriateness through different lenses. For example, sharing images and revealing sexual orientation on social media were viewed as more acceptable by medical students than by medical faculty and public participants (A. Jain et al., 2014).

Use of screening or using information gleaned from Internet searches for graduate school, practicum, internship, postdoctoral, or hiring decisions raises a number of ethical and legal issues. There has been a diminution of the line between private and professional identity. Previously, supervisors and supervisees alike believed each could limit disclosure of personal data though personal intentional acts such as having no personal pictures in one's office and not wearing a wedding ring. However, the Internet era has brought a high level of transparency and visibility of therapist behavior revealed through Google searches, social networks, and listservs (Zur, Williams, Lehavot, & Knapp, 2009). Psychologist and physician training sites are using search engines and social networking sites to screen applicants for professionalism (S. H. Jain, 2009; Wester, Danforth, & Olle, 2013), and many are requiring Facebook passwords as part of the application process (Schulman, Kuchkarian, Withum, Boecker, & Graygo, 2013) although some states have legislated that to be illegal (Stinson, 2014). Although informed consent for information placed on the web is assumed when information is posted, should information culled from Internet searches be used in high-stakes decisions? Consider (a) whether there was a reasonable expectation of privacy, (b) whether the information is credible and reliable, (c) whether the information was hearsay if one has no ability to assess or ascertain trustworthiness (Wester et al., 2013; M. S. Zohn, personal communication, August 21, 2013).

Legal peril exists with heightened scrutiny under the 14th Amendment Equal Protection Clause and antidiscrimination laws. There is strict scrutiny for "suspect classifications" (e.g., race, national origin, religion). If it were determined that an Internet search identified a suspect classification, it could be argued that that was the reason for not accepting the trainee for the position (Wester et al., 2013; M. S. Zohn, personal communication, August 21, 2013).

Thinking of social networks proactively, work with supervisees to collaboratively assess potential for establishment of social media for professional purposes, clinical departments, or research centers; foster dissemination of psychological knowledge; and enhance health care and general information provided to the public (George & Green, 2012). Rather than focusing on the negative and ethical peril, we have to draw our supervisees into a discussion of strengths and new benefits. Already, the first place most individuals seek out medical information is the Web (Fox & Duggan, 2013). Assessment and ongoing attention to skills and attitudes and discrepancies between supervisors who may be less Internet savvy and supervisees are essential. This may represent a tilt of the hierarchy of supervision and presents an excellent opportunity for collaboration.

REGULATORY ISSUES FOR TELEPSYCHOLOGY

In addition to being responsible for competence under the laws and regulations of the state or provincial government in which the practice is being supervised (and knowledge of the legality of practicing, even briefly, when the client is in another jurisdiction), the supervisor also bears responsibility for knowledge of regulations regarding supervision for that jurisdiction and for referring the supervisee for guidance regarding regulations and requirements for licensure in jurisdictions in which they plan to practice in the future (e.g., Association of State and Provincial Psychology Boards [ASPPB] website: http://www.asppb.net). For example, in a tally of disciplinary actions taken by psychology boards, improper or inadequate supervision or delegation is in the top ten sanctioned practices (DeMers & Schaffer, 2012). Such regulations get even more complex in the context of telepsychology. *Guidelines for the Practice of Telepsychology* (APA, 2013) were developed by a joint task force established by the APA, the ASPPB, and the APA Insurance Trust. The guidelines balance the competence of the psychologist who provides or oversees telepsychology technologies with the need to ensure the client is fully aware of the risks, limitations, and challenges of security and confidentiality. The guidelines address the competence of the psychologist, standards of care in the delivery of telepsychology services, informed consent, confidentiality of data and information, security of data and information, disposal of data and information and technologies, testing and assessment, and interjurisdictional practice.

TELEPSYCHOLOGY SUPERVISION

An abundance of direct clinical services can be provided through telepsychology, and supervision may be provided by this means as well. Several types of technology are available: videoconference, cloud based file-sharing software, and clinical outcomes tracking software (Rousmaniere, Abbass, & Frederickson, 2014). Although studies of supervision via videoconferencing have been conducted and the practice is increasing, providing access to individuals in training and practice in remote areas, which reduces isolation and provides specialized input and consultation, it is still necessary for supervision to have an in-person component (Barnett, 2011).

Some barriers to the effectiveness of telesupervision include inability to respond to emotional reactivity of the supervisee, level of supervisee disclosure, potential for more formulaic format, and lack of access for the supervisor to contextual or emerging issues in the distant site where the client contact is occurring. Reese and colleagues (2009) reported that for a small sample and short supervision interval, limited visual cues led to enhanced verbal communication while showing some indication that advanced students were more satisfied than novices with the videoconferencing modality. Also, Reese's subjects confirmed that the more formulaic format was easier and thus more desirable, raising for us the concern that ease and comfort are not necessarily desirable outcomes of supervision. The challenge of growth-oriented supervision as a process leading to independent practice is often uncomfortable and challenging when attempting to ensure that supervisees confront personal issues that are informing the clinical process. We concur with Deane, Gonsalvez, Blackman, Saffioti, and Andresen (2015) that an essential part of any telesupervision is the telesupervisor having access to videos of the therapist–client sessions during the telesupervision session. We support the use of the model proposed by Abbass and colleagues (2011) for video review as an essential part of telesupervision in enhancing reflection and that of Deane and colleagues (2015), an e-supervision platform that includes a video annotation tool to shape metacompetencies and support relationship management, portending future platforms with greater potential.

The *Guidelines for the Practice of Telepsychology* (APA, 2013) encourage supervisors to consult with those who are knowledgeable about the unique issues posed, strive to be familiar with the professional literature, have competence with provision of technology, and ensure that adequate face-to-face supervision is included to confirm that the supervisees reach the requisite competence.

SUMMARY

Competency-based clinical supervision requires ethics, and ethics require competence. Both the conduct of clinical supervision and the services rendered under supervision involve careful consideration and application of law and ethics. Competency-based clinical supervision is uniquely suited to facilitate training in this task through its emphasis on assembling and integrating into practice knowledge (of law and ethics), skills (in applying law and ethics using reasoned and accepted decision-making processes), and attitudes (consistent with the principles and ethics of the APA, 2010, and other professional standards). Rather than focusing solely on violations (and on extreme breaches of law and ethics), we advocate emphasis on the daily, ever-present practice of ethics and application of law and the creation of an ethical community of practitioners and supervisors from whom supervisees can learn and become socialized into a culture exemplifying the highest principles and standards of the profession.

7

Supervisees Who Do Not Meet Professional Competence Standards

Supervisees who do not meet professional competence standards present a difficult problem for supervisors, one that has been referred to as the "hot potato" of clinical training (Johnson et al., 2008). The situation is complex, given the supervisor's multiple obligations to clients, the profession, the public, graduate schools and training institutions, and the supervisee. In addition, supervisors must be clear about their expectations for supervisee performance and be able to make distinctions between normative developmental challenges and failures to meet competence standards.

Supervisees who do not meet professional competence standards have been described in multiple ways—as supervisees with performance problems or trainees with problems of professional competence who demonstrate behaviors, attitudes, and/or skills that are not consistent with

http://dx.doi.org/10.1037/15962-007
Supervision Essentials for the Practice of Competency-Based Supervision, by C. A. Falender and E. P. Shafranske

expected ethical or professional standards given their stage of training (Elman & Forrest, 2007). They exhibit

> interference in professional functioning that is reflected in one or more of the following ways: (a) an inability and/or unwillingness to acquire and integrate professional standards into one's repertoire of professional behavior, (b) an inability to acquire professional skills in order to reach an acceptable level of competency, and (c) an inability to control personal stress, psychological dysfunction, and/or excessive emotional reactions that interfere with professional functioning. (Lamb, Presser, Pfost, Baum, Jackson, & Jarvis, 1987, p. 598)

Further,

> (a) [The supervisee] does not acknowledge, understand, or address the problem when it is identified, (b) the problem is not merely a reflection of a skill deficit that can be rectified by academic or didactic training, (c) the quality of services delivered . . . is consistently negatively affected, (d) the problem is not restricted to one area of professional functioning, (e) a disproportionate amount of attention by training personnel is required, and/or (f) the . . . behavior does not change as a function of feedback, remediation efforts, and/or time. (Lamb et al., 1987, p. 599)

The *Guidelines for Clinical Supervision in Health Service Psychology* (American Psychological Association, 2014) address specific roles for supervisors addressing professional competence problems:

- Supervisors understand and adhere both to the supervisory contract and to program, institutional, and legal policies and procedures related to performance evaluations.
- Supervisors strive to address performance problems directly.
- Supervisors strive to identify potential performance problems promptly, communicate these to the supervisee, and take steps to address these in a timely manner allowing for opportunities to effect change.
- Supervisors are competent in developing and implementing plans to remediate performance problems.

- Supervisors are mindful of their role as gatekeeper and take appropriate and ethical action in response to supervisee performance problems. (pp. 21–23)

Unfortunately, supervisors may avoid difficult conversations or even informing the supervisee of areas of competence that do not meet criteria, whether they be competency benchmarks (Fouad et al., 2009; Hatcher et al., 2013), other competency criteria, or specialty performance standards (e.g., for the specialty Forensics; Varela & Conroy, 2012). Supervisors call on their own values and commitments to professionalism and their knowledge and skills to faithfully fulfill the obligations to address problems in competence.

Some of the practices essential to performance monitoring include ensuring that every supervisee views him- or herself as in development, incorporates ongoing feedback, and is aware of how developing competencies correspond to the setting's expectations. Competency-based supervision is particularly well suited to preventing competence problems and to addressing those that arise early. Most effective is combining supervisee self-assessment with ongoing tracking and monitoring collaboration between supervisor and supervisee. Supervisor transparency, providing feedback to the supervisee when the supervisor notes an area of lesser competence or any knowledge, skill, or attitude that worries the supervisor or is a competence issue, is ethically and legally essential because it provides an assurance for the supervisee that the area(s) in question will be addressed and the trainee with have the opportunity to grow, develop, and increase competency.

Ideally, areas of lesser competency are addressed immediately when observed (or shortly thereafter) rather than when the supervisor provides a virtual laundry list of deficiencies after observing and accumulating these over an extended time interval. Providing so much accumulated feedback without any previous attention or notice places the supervisee at a distinct disadvantage and may be overwhelming. The supervisee may feel hopeless.

An essential part of identifying supervisees with professional competence problems is to seek collegial consultation before proceeding. If there are multiple supervisors, ascertain whether other supervisors perceive the same competence problems and, if not, explore with the other supervisors what they identify as areas of competence. Consider whether there are differences related to the demand characteristics of the practice area (e.g., assessment vs. psychotherapy; child and family work vs. adult) and the supervisory relationship. It is incumbent on the supervisor to ensure that the problem identified is not specific to the particular interaction with the one supervisor rather than a more generalized competence problem. If the former is true, consider whether the problem is in the formation of the supervisory alliance or relationship, whether there has been such an alliance but it has become strained or ruptured, or whether there has been an impasse. Those issues should be addressed, after which the supervisor should reassess and consult about whether there is also a competence problem. Essential components of dealing with competence problems include the following:

- Provide early feedback and documentation. Define specific behaviors that do not meet professional competence standards or criteria. It is essential that the feedback on competencies is anchored in the supervisee's collaborative self-assessment and ongoing monitoring of specific competencies (e.g., benchmarks or another competency frame) that have been formally introduced to the supervisee and that the processes of collaboratively identifying appropriate goals has been completed. There should be no surprises in feedback or competencies.
- Ensure that you have distinguished between normative developmental challenges and competence problems.
- Do not use the word *impairment* to refer to supervisee competence problems. Use of that word invokes the Americans With Disabilities Act. (ADA). *Impairment* has been preempted by that act and refers to an individual with mental or physical disabilities. If you use the word, you are indicating that you perceive the individual supervisee as having such disabilities, and you are violating the law by not proceeding with reasonable accommodations. Instead of the word *impairment*, state the specific competencies and behaviors that are not meeting performance standards (Falender, Collins, & Shafranske, 2009). (Please note the supervisee's action of invoking the ADA is a strength.)

- Ensure good and specific feedback as early as possible on performance areas.
- Consult and collaborate with the school, training director/administrative head, and personnel or human resources department to ensure due process and compliance with all personnel practices.
- Propose an early remediation plan: Develop a plan to enhance each area of competence, considering the contribution of knowledge, skills, and attitudes/value components in the discussion and plan (use the Competency Remediation Plan template retrieved from http://www.apa.org/ed/graduate/competency.aspx).
- Develop specific, measurable steps to assist development, anchoring each step to specific competency areas.
- Engage in difficult conversations regarding contextual or other issues. Consider the importance of cultural, diversity, and contextual factors. Consider the interaction of the client, supervisee, and supervisor's worldviews and how these affect the competence problem.
- Monitor and track performance on a timeline with multiple and ongoing check-ins.
- Once you have begun competence monitoring and tracking, continue to monitor at set (less frequent) intervals, even after the supervisee has achieved suitable competence gains (elaborated from Falender, Collins, & Shafranske, 2009; Forrest et al., 2013).

Supervisees who do not meet professional competence standards pose significant challenges and invoke particular responsibilities for the supervisor. Attitudes, knowledge, and skills conjoin with professionalism and contribute to the supervisor's ability to address situations in which performance standards are not being met. Keeping in mind his or her multiple obligations, supervisors engage with transparency, clearly articulating performance expectations at the beginning of supervision, establishing behaviorally anchored indicators of performance and directly communicating concerns, and providing direction when observing competence problems. Supervisors use best practices when providing feedback, developing remediation plans, monitoring progress, and gatekeeping.

8

Becoming a Supervisor and Enhancing Supervisor Expertise

From a competency-based perspective, the moment a supervisee begins in the role of supervisee, he or she is beginning training to become a supervisor (Falender & Shafranske, 2012a), although such experience is never sufficient preparation to conduct supervision. The first step is to become an effective supervisee, learning the various aspects of the supervision process and engaging in role induction (Falender & Shafranske, 2012a; Vespia, Heckman-Stone, & Delworth, 2002) such that the aspects of the supervisee's role and expectations are carefully addressed and understood.

http://dx.doi.org/10.1037/15962-008
Supervision Essentials for the Practice of Competency-Based Supervision, by C. A. Falender and E. P. Shafranske

ROLE INVOCATION FROM THE PERSPECTIVE OF THE SUPERVISEE

The first step is thinking back to one's own experience as a supervisee, considering the sections derived from the Supervisor Utilization Rating Form (Vespia et al., 2002, as cited in Falender & Shafranske, 2012a) as role induction. To assess one's competence as a supervisee, consider

- your attitudes, preparation, and willingness to grow;
- your view of the supervision process (i.e., active, passive, goal oriented, collaborative);
- your ability to admit to difficulties or to discuss errors;
- your skill at discussing issues or problems with the supervisory relationship and to self-critique;
- your openness to feedback, accepting it nondefensively, and giving feedback to the supervisor;
- your understanding of how personal dynamics relate to psychotherapy and supervision, as evidenced by speaking openly about personal and emotional responses to clients; and
- your openness to multiple perspectives, client ratings of outcomes, and ethical and legal perspectives.

ROLE INVOCATION AS A SUPERVISOR

It is important for the supervisor-in-training to engage in role invocation with the supervisee and to include the expectations and ground rules of the supervisor role, essentially adopting the "supervisor" stance in role invocation, starting with such basics as the format for supervision; what the supervisor-in-training should prepare and have available in terms of written, audio, or video materials; two-way feedback expectations; multicultural and diversity competence and infusion in the supervision process, ethical, legal, and site regulations; and general expectations, such as being interactive and coming to supervision prepared. The supervisor-in-training has to think of specific, contextually driven expectations for the supervisee. Thorough role invocation is an essential part of the establishment of the supervisory relationship.

With the recognition that supervision is an exquisite balance of the power differential and collaboration with the supervisee, it is a dynamic process. The supervisor has to communicate to the supervisee a sense of empowerment to learn, grow, and collaborate to ensure his or her needs are addressed as much as is possible within the context that the supervision occurs. At the same time, the supervisor is responsible for socializing the supervisee to fully understand the complexity and art of the supervisor role: balancing the highest duty of protection for the client with gate-keeping for the profession, ensuring that only suitable candidates move forward, and fostering and enhancing the development of the supervisee's self-awareness and competence.

The supervisor holds significant power and typically is privileged as well, having a secure job, income, and status. The supervisor should be mindful that, in contrast, to obtain their doctorate supervisees may be financially challenged with significant debt. History of oppression may also increase the power differential. Attending to power and privilege and supervisee perspectives is an essential part of the supervisor's role negotiating the power differential with the supervisee.

The process of transitioning into the supervisory role is a complex one. Multiple authors have addressed the stages of development (summarized in Falender & Shafranske, 2004), with some consensus that beginning supervisors experience role shock and may feel like imposters—one day (in some states) they were supervisees and the next day, supervisors. They may also be acutely worried about vicarious liability, stating, "I worked too hard to earn my own license; I'm not going to jeopardize it with some trainee." With experience, the supervisor moves toward greater confidence, less crisis orientation, more graceful acceptance of supervisee feedback, and greater competence. Sadly, studies have not incorporated the impact of training in clinical supervision, from our perspective a sine qua non of practice.

STAGES OF SUPERVISOR DEVELOPMENT

Although there has been limited to no empirical support beyond experiential validity for the developmental theories of supervisee and supervisor development, there has been a resurgence of interest in the topic.

Goodyear, Lichtenberg, Bang, and Gragg (2014) elaborated on 10 changes psychotherapists undergo as they become supervisors:

1. Becoming able to perceive/act on complex response opportunities.
2. Learning to think like a supervisor.
3. Developing the ability to be oneself.
4. Learning to view one's self as a supervisor.
5. Developing the capacity to use reflection as a tool to monitor one's biases and one's impact on others.
6. Developing confidence in one's judgments about what constitutes effective counseling.
7. Developing confidence in one's competence as a supervisor.
8. Developing patience with the process of supervisee development.
9. Developing the courage to do the right thing in the gatekeeper role.
10. Learning to understand and manage power. (p. 1044)

These steps correspond nicely with a competency-based approach to clinical supervision and with the American Psychological Association (APA; 2014, 2015) *Guidelines for Clinical Supervision in Health Service Psychology*. Additional empirical research on the developmental stage model is required, as is consideration of changes in clinicians' use of knowledge, skills, and attitudes in making the transition to supervisors.

HOW TO: THE TRAINING MODULES

For supervisor training during graduate school, a first step is a proseminar. Training in the supervisor role should progress after the supervisee has obtained significant competence in his or her own clinical skills and competencies. Falender, Burnes, and Ellis (2013) recommended that doctoral programs require a self-contained sequence of coursework in clinical supervision, coursework that supervisees wish they could have (Crook-Lyon, Presnell, Silva, Suyama, & Stickney, 2011). At the onset of clinical training, supervisees are taught the essentials of clinical supervision, engage in role invocation to become a supervisee and understand the complexity of the process, and are empowered in their role as supervisees (Falender & Shafranske, 2012a). Next, after completing a minimum

2-year practicum in which they practice peer supervision, they begin study and practice for the transition from supervisee to supervisor.

In this section, we highlight a training model that I (CF) use in training supervisors. The course introduces supervisees to the supervision literature, models, and competency-based supervision using exercises and activities to experience the perspective of the supervisor and the significant cognitive shift from being a supervisee. Supervisors in training learn knowledge, skills, and attitudes to ensure effective supervision practice. In conjunction with focused reading assignments from texts (i.e., Bernard & Goodyear, 2014; Falender & Shafranske, 2004, 2012a), task force guidelines for supervision (APA, 2014, 2015; Association of State and Provincial Psychology Boards, 2015), and selected readings on current research findings in the field, supervisees engage in discussion and activities to conceptualize the knowledge, skills, and attitudes/values that constitute supervisor competence and begin the career-long process of self-assessment of their supervisory competence.

Then supervisees role-play in "supervisor–supervisee" dyads with peers. The role-plays correspond to supervision of supervisees with complex client presentations, including clinical and multicultural diversity intersections. The organization of themes provides an ideal sounding board for the supervisees to gain perspective and confidence and to reflect on their own supervision experience as they begin to internalize the role of supervisor themselves. A senior supervisor oversees the process. Topics include establishing the supervisory relationship and the contract, dealing with strains and ruptures and their repair, managing countertransference or reactivity, dealing with legal and ethical issues, and dealing with the intersection of all of these with client clinical presentations that include multicultural diversity (e.g., socioeconomic status, age, religion, sexual orientation, gender identity, immigration).

ROLE TRANSITION

The supervisee's role has been a combination of action and dependency, with the comfort of knowing that the supervisor is ultimately responsible and that the supervisor is available and ready to assist, support, direct, or intervene as necessary. Kaslow and Bell (2008) referred to this as the "holding environment" (p. 19), à la Winnicott (1986), foundational for the beginning supervisee and associated with development of a professional identity separate both from previous supervisors and from other authority figures in their lives. Developing a collaborative relationship with the supervisee within the construct of the power differential may pose a challenge to some supervisors in training. Reference to feminist supervision literature may serve to pave the way for supervisors in development who find the role perplexing. Brown (2016), Porter and Vasquez (1997), and Vargas, Porter, and Falender (2008) provided guidance and examples of the development of a respectful, collaborative relationship with the supervisee within the transparent power differential. Development of the supervisory alliance is facilitated by encouragement of mutual self-reflection and examination by modeling receptivity, authenticity, openness, and respect.

As supervisees in the seminar prepare the role-plays, they adopt the perspective of supervisor and synthesize the readings on the particular focal chapters from *Multiculturalism and Diversity in Clinical Supervision: A Competency-Based Approach* (Falender, Shafranske, & Falicov, 2014). The integration of evidence, competencies, and creative problem solving as well as the reflections and feedback from peers in the group provides for greater depth of understanding, enhanced empathy for the supervisor, and the beginning of the emergence of a professional sense of supervisor identity. A particular challenge is integrating multiple supervisor responsibilities: fostering supervisee insight, growth, and competent practice while protecting the patient (including making difficult decisions about whether continuing this client practice may do harm) and monitoring supervisee practice or lack of such. They weigh the developmentally normative behaviors against those that require remedial action.

EXAMPLES

The following are examples from the supervision role-plays. One supervisee assumes the role of supervisor and the other of supervisee, but they both engage in a reflective process to gain perspective on each. The course instructor and metasupervisor (CF) provided additional reflection on and input to the process.

The supervisee had been seeing a client for four sessions when the client revealed that she was bisexual and was wondering whether she should tell her boyfriend of several months. This disclosure prompted a raft of emotional responses from the supervisee/therapist: surprise, distress, a feeling of being overwhelmed, and general alarm, as well as awe that the client trusted her to make such a disclosure. The supervisee ended the session about 15 minutes early, saying she needed to get supervision on this. She cited her own lack of experience with sexual orientation and her profound fear of working with that client. The supervisor first reflected on multiple aspects of response. Her first impulse was to jump right into telling the supervisee what to do, but that impulse was quickly replaced by a decision to take a reflective stance and address the supervisee/therapist's response, potential impact on client, and how the personal response and emotional reaction informed the supervisee's behavior. The supervisor reflected on how easy it would be to condemn the supervisee without giving her a chance to process and deconstruct her response and the impact on the client. By disclosing "fear," the supervisee opened a door to examination and growth. And the "awe" at the power and trust in the disclosure was a critical factor. A fascinating revelation was the multiple levels of vulnerability and the potential through a respectful process to bridge the supervisee/therapist's transition from emotion to reflection and insight. The supervisor was warm and empathic and elicited a more nuanced response from the supervisee, opening the door to exploring how and whether this particular supervisee could or should proceed with the client. The dyad reflected on how their own personal religious and belief structures were relevant and how they had to frame responses in supervisor responsibility to the client and the profession. Ultimately, the supervisor collaborated with the larger group to brainstorm possible avenues to proceed, remaining respectful of the supervisee's personal beliefs but empowering her to enlist worldview inclusivity (Bieschke & Mintz, 2012). The supervisee was empowered to reflect on the awe and to continue to explore her experience and ideas for moving forward. The supervisor felt empowered to lead this process with the supervisee and was appreciative of the openness and vulnerability of that supervisee. Supervisees reported these exercises provided an opportunity to experience the intensity of the moment and to gain greater understanding of the role change.

In the next example, the supervisee described a 36-year-old female client who was unmarried and unpartnered and who was struggling with relationship issues. The supervisor told the supervisee that the critical issue that the client should be worried about was the ticking of her biological clock. The supervisee was surprised because that was not an issue the client had presented, but the supervisor insisted it had to be the central focus. The supervisee tried to gently suggest alternatives to the supervisor, reflecting on how personal factors can influence one's perspective and restating what the client indicated unequivocally as the reason for seeking therapy: her difficulty establishing a relationship. The group then reflected on circumstances when they felt that supervisor worldviews had directed supervision interactions, their efforts to forestall or redirect while remaining mindful that their own worldviews were affecting all the interactions, and their concern for client protection.

In a role-play on the collaborative approach to feedback, the supervisor described the normative nature of feedback and asked the supervisee to describe previous feedback received and how it was framed to be most effective. The supervisee responded that she had difficulty with feedback because it reminded her of her critical parents. The supervisor said that that must be difficult but persisted, explaining this it was an excellent opportunity to identify ways that feedback could be useful and accepted. The supervisor urged the supervisee to identify an area in which she thought she might receive feedback, and the supervisee offered that she was sometimes too tentative with clients in interactions, possibly because she was afraid she would hurt their feelings if she intervened. The metasupervisor (CF) reflected that that might be an interesting possible parallel process and that it was important to address. The supervisee was surprised, but on reflection agreed. With the intent of facilitating experiential learning, the metasupervisor recommended that they reverse roles and engage in a role-play to examine further the dynamics. The supervisee played the role of supervisor and suggested (tentatively) that it seemed like the supervisee was lacking in confidence when she intervened with a particular client. The supervisee agreed, saying that interventions were so "certain" that she wondered what would happen if they were wrong. The supervisor suggested that that might be a feeling arising from inexperience and that with increased experience and success, the supervisee might feel more certain, but to reach that point, she would have to begin to take a few risks under supervision to begin to see the impact.

In another role-play, the supervisee was worried about receiving feedback. He repeatedly asked not to be given feedback because it interfered with his ability to grow. The supervisor reflectively and gently described her duty to the client and explained that feedback is not interference, but a pathway to growth. Through a series of approximations, the supervisor gave specific, competency-based feedback on strengths and areas in development, including the ability to receive feedback. The supervisor reflected how difficult it was to give feedback to someone who wanted none and how it highlighted the transformation and the role as well as the power to protect the client. Other students in the group suggested the use of outcome measures for the client (Grossl, Reese, Norsworthy, & Hopkins, 2014) and for the supervisee (Tsong & Goodyear, 2014; Worthen & Lambert, 2007) to track performance and to use those to scale and calibrate supervisee feedback, modeling how the supervisee can give progress outcome data back to the client.

In another role-play, the supervisee appeared depressed and despondent and described how upset he had been about the severe suicidal ideation of a client. The supervisor, attempting not to react too strongly asked when this occurred and why he had not contacted her immediately. He said he was just into his own process and felt there were some personal issues he had to deal with regarding suicidality before he could deal with the client or take it to the supervisor. The supervisor described the flood of responses: her highest duty to protect the client, the fear it might be too late, the need for immediate contact with the client to arrange for a session in the next hour, sitting in with the supervisee, whether she had adequately determined the supervisee's level of competence to deal with a suicidal client, and whether she had described the emergency plan necessary in such a case. On reflection, it became clear that the issue was whether her own incompetence as a supervisor was to blame and whether it was necessary to write up a performance plan, identifying the competence areas that were severely deficient—especially understanding that the highest duty of the therapist and the supervisor is to protect the client and that not doing so is illegal and dramatically outside the standard of practice. This was reinforced by the metasupervisor (CF) who agreed about the difficulty of the supervisor's roles in protecting the client, enforcing and monitoring ethical and legal standards, and gatekeeping for the profession while still maintaining a strong supervisory relationship. The metasupervisor emphasized that the highest duty is protection of the client; this particular interaction served to accentuate that duty for the supervisor and emphasize that it is a developmental transition to understand and act on that duty.

Throughout each session, the group reflected on the intersection of competence issues in which knowledge and skills were low, but felt that attitude, including some reactivity, was salient. They also reflected on how difficult it sometimes felt to give feedback to supervisees and to make decisions about protecting the client and about supervisee gatekeeping. The group found role-playing within the role-play to be effective: The supervisor and supervisee in the role-play planfully switched roles and considered alternative strategies and perspectives. Also, they frequently assigned targeted readings (i.e., managing countertransference and personal factors; Falender & Shafranske, 2004, Chapter 4). They reported that through the role-plays they gained greater perspective on the importance of the supervisory alliance, examination of personal beliefs and attitudes in the context of diversity competence, how this process is normalized, and management of supervisor and supervisee reactivity, and they decided they felt that video review of sessions was an essential and invaluable tool in supervision, giving depth, nuance, and access to behavioral segments from which to anchor supervisee feedback.

The next step in the development of supervisor competence includes ongoing supervision of supervision groups. In these, the focus is on expansion of supervisor skills, knowledge, and attitudes through targeted reading, video review, and feedback. Finally, a supervision consultation group in which supervisors bring dilemmas or successes to the group to demonstrate their growth or ask for input on supervision practice plays an important role in the professional development of a supervisor. A rotating system of bringing topical journal articles and providing review of these for the group enhances knowledge.

The concept of the moving target of competence requires that supervisors frequently step back and reflect on their supervision, their areas of strength, and areas that they or others have identified as being in development. Openness to input from peers is a critical aspect of supervisor development. Self-assessment is a step in development and one that contributes a communitarian culture of competence (Johnson, Barnett, Elman, Forrest, & Kaslow, 2013).

9

Transforming Clinical Supervision

The past decade has inaugurated an era of competence, an era that brings both opportunities and challenges. The scope of change needed is great and requires a reconfiguration of research and practice. A starting point is further operationalizing definitions of competence because the view of competence as an end state obscures the day-to-day reality that clinicians and supervisors must continuously self-assess and enhance their skills to respond to the clinical needs of their patients and the training needs of their supervisees. How do we measure supervisory competence? And how do we conduct education and training in clinical supervision not only to establish a threshold of competence but also to encourage ongoing development? When is the best time to train psychologists in the practice of clinical supervision: during graduate school, internship, or postdoctoral training? How do we ensure that

http://dx.doi.org/10.1037/15962-009
Supervision Essentials for the Practice of Competency-Based Supervision, by C. A. Falender and E. P. Shafranske

such training does occur, and how do we assess ongoing supervisor competence? These are not just academic but also imminently practical questions.

We have to understand better the barriers to transforming supervision (e.g., attitudes toward value and utility of supervision, lack of familiarity with current theories and research of supervision) and identify ways to ensure the implementation of competency-based clinical supervision. Efforts to advance the quality of clinical supervision should be initiated at all levels of the training community and in the health care system to ensure public welfare. Supervisors, despite their best efforts, are often so burdened with high clinical caseloads and professional responsibilities that clinical supervision suffers. Initiatives should be undertaken to establish public policy and standards that ensure the provision of the highest quality of supervision. It is only through concerted efforts in education, training, research, and practice that clinical supervision will fulfill its obligations to the public, the profession, and to future generations of health service psychologists.

As we have set forth in our writings, competency-based clinical supervision provides an orientation to competence and a systematic approach and invites a degree of face validity; however, much work is still required to validate scientifically its effectiveness and to identify best practices in its dissemination.

Implicit in the transformation to competency-based supervision is the need for systematic research on supervisor competence as linked to effectiveness of practices and approaches prescribed in competency-based clinical supervision. The development of valid and reliable measures of clinical competence and supervisor competence, including the monitoring of clinical performance, will enhance accountability of the clinical process and supervision. Similarly, research is needed to examine the effects of the use of specific supervision interventions on the effects and outcomes of supervision as well as on clinical outcomes (Falender, 2014). Self-report measures, the most prevalent ones used currently, will not suffice. Mixed method research will be valuable in examining the nuances and subjective experiences of participants as well as the efficacy of the procedures. Single subject research, investigating the impact of supervision interventions on clinical performance by studying the session-by-session impact of feedback on supervisee clinical behavior, is a particularly useful method to capture the effects of supervision interventions. Advances in translational research, which intentionally brings well-designed scientific investigations based in research settings into dialog with real world practice, offer the possibility of advancing competency-based clinical supervision by focusing on challenges in implementation. Whereas research attention has been dedicated to the supervisory relationship (e.g., Inman et al., 2014), more has to be learned about what leads to effective supervisory relationships and the supervisory working alliance, including the use of the competency-based model as well as the systematic study of the multiple components of supervision (American Psychological Association [APA], 2014, 2015). We also need to know what does not work as well as what does and the consequences inadequate or harmful supervision has for the client.

The cultural change required to transform clinical supervision practice to the era of competence and evidence-based practice will require significant effort. Changes must occur in knowledge, skills, and attitudes of supervisors and supervisees. The transformation is heralded by the *Guidelines for Clinical Supervision in Health Service Psychology* (APA, 2014, 2015), accreditation, and regulation (Association of State and Provincial Psychology Boards, 2015), all of which are competency-based. In addition, multiple international jurisdictions have adopted competency-based approaches (Gonsalvez & Calvert, 2014).

However, barriers to change exist, and overcoming these requires a systematic, system-wide approach. For example, changes can be implemented at the system level, in which the foundation approach to clinical supervision is transformed, or they may occur at the individual level, in which the practice of supervision is tailored to the unique training needs of the supervisee or to address strains or difficulties in the supervisory relationship, affecting its effectiveness. In both circumstances, thoughtful consideration is required to ensure that the oversight and training responsibilities are met as delineated in the supervision contract.

SYSTEM CHANGE TO COMPETENCY-BASED SUPERVISION

The transformation to competency-based supervision requires a mind shift as well as self-assessment and active change. Simply adopting a supervision model (e.g., psychotherapy-based, developmental) is not sufficient. An essential element of competency-based supervision is the systematic approach to the component parts: supervisory alliance or relationship formation; supervision contract; diversity and personal factors; assessment, evaluation, and feedback; ethics, legal, and regulatory issues; and professionalism. Not all these elements are included in individual supervision models. Thus, competency-based supervision, a metatheoretical approach, is essential in the systems transformation.

TRANSFORMATION OF SUPERVISION AT THE PROGRAM LEVEL

At the program level, the transformation requires the supervisor to be a transformational leader. Change in programs or individual functioning is difficult, and this change is no different. It is useful to consider readiness of the setting/milieu to change, a process facilitated by transparent and overt assessment. Transformational leadership skills (Kaslow, Falender, & Grus, 2012) empower a leader to address some of the pressing mental health and training needs (e.g., burnout, stress, lack of motivation), address readiness to change, and develop a vision of supportive, lifelong learning in which each individual, supervisors and supervisees alike, has an individual plan for growth and development with goals and tasks. It also entails developing the knowledge, skills, and attitudes requisite for competency-based supervision, ensuring that all members of the organizational structure value the importance of competency-based supervision as a lifelong learning strategy.

Building on existing or emerging practices of supervision already in place, team members are encouraged to use unique personal strengths or interests, create momentum for growth, and provide support and reinforcement through the energy and enthusiasm generated in the process.

As each staff member feels empowered to change, a culture shift occurs. Kotter (1996) described stages of change beginning with (a) establishing a sense of urgency, which in this case could relate to prevention of burnout or preparation for accreditation; (b) creating a guiding coalition or a core group of supervisors who share the momentum to change; (c) developing a vision and a strategy including the benefits of competency-based supervision; (d) communicating the vision; (e) empowering broad-based action; (f) generating short-term wins or successes and highlighting those; (g) consolidating gains; and (h) anchoring in the culture, ensuring institutional buy-in across the setting.

Transformation in clinical supervision involves multiple levels of both supervisor and supervisee change. First, for supervisors, change entails (a) identifying, practicing, transmitting, and ensuring implementation of the skills, knowledge, and attitudes for the practice of effective clinical supervision and effective assessment and monitoring of the supervisee; (b) instilling motivation for the change to competency-based practice in individuals and throughout the setting; (c) providing specialized training for supervisors in clinical supervision to foster the change from supervision through osmosis to one guided by formalized practice; and (d) addressing the complexity of the supervisor responsibilities to clients, supervisees, training institutions, laws and regulations, and the tensions that may arise from the multiple functions performed in supervision. In addition, supervisors ensure compliance of staff and supervisees with agency regulations while promoting everyone's professional development. These multiple roles create potential tensions between supportive interactions and evaluation or gatekeeping (i.e., supervisor judgment of supervisee competence) functions.

For supervisees, change entails (a) being initiated into the era of competency-based education, including specialized training and readings (Hatcher et al., 2013); (b) supporting the supervisee in self-assessment, understanding the chronic poor self-assessment skills of psychologists and other mental health professionals (Dunning, Heath, & Suls, 2004); (c) assisting in translating areas of developing competence into goals for supervision and the corresponding tasks for supervisee and supervisor;

and (d) supporting the collaborative monitoring of the development of goals for supervision as they progress in meeting the criterion-referenced competence standards (e.g., competency benchmarks) and revising and updating those as they are achieved.

On the supervisee–supervisor level, competency-based supervision also requires changes. It entails a systematic approach based on the assessment of competence of the supervisee. Supervision is experiential in nature and is highly interactive. By *experiential*, we are referring to use of multiple techniques, including role-playing client–therapist interactions, with the supervisor switching roles with the supervisee from client to therapist; practicing skills; modeling by the supervisor; and using ethical decision-making models, all practices associated with enhanced client outcomes (Bearman et al., 2013).

The concept of the moving target of competence requires that supervisors frequently step back and reflect on their supervision, their areas of strength, and areas that they or others have identified as being in development. Openness to input from peers is a critical aspect of supervisor development. Self-assessment is a step toward a communitarian culture of competence proposed by Johnson, Barnett, Elman, Forrest, and Kaslow (2013) and Johnson et al. (2014). They proposed creating a communitarian culture/community of competence, a concept that will be powerful for supervisors to model and instill in supervisees. They proposed development of a culture of authenticity and self-awareness with the potential for supervisors to model

- *access to and expression of one's thoughts and feelings.* Supervisors could model other-oriented empathy or the ability to understand others' experiences and perspectives and a genuine concern for the welfare of others.
- *accepting vulnerability and nondefensiveness.* Supervisors would admit the limitations of one's knowledge, skill, and attitudes, combined with an openness to help and to give feedback without marked loss of self-esteem.
- *engaging in self-care and the ability to model personal health and emotional well-being* (Norcross & Guy, 2005).

- *acknowledging fluid expertise*—the ability to transition easily from expert to learner to allow mutual influence and to maximize collaboration.
- *initiating and accepting collegial assertiveness*—the ability to initiate difficult conversations as an expression of care (Jacobs et al., 2011), a desire to deepen the relationship, and a commitment to promote one's own and collegial competence.

Further, Johnson et al. (2013, 2014) urged the formation of competence constellations: an inner core or a small nucleus of mentors and colleagues who know the individual well and are not afraid to give corrective as well as supportive feedback. A larger constellation is composed of more varied contacts who provide a wide spectrum of input, connection, stimulation, and fun. Engaging in all these steps and culture changes will assist in the transformation to competency-based supervision and a mind-set of continuous growth, development, self-challenge, and energy.

Recommended Readings

Barnett, J. E., & Molzon, C. H. (2014). Clinical supervision of psychotherapy: Essential ethics issues for supervisors and supervisees. *Journal of Clinical Psychology, 70,* 1051–1061. http://dx.doi.org/10.1002/jclp.22126

As suggested by the title, this article provides a succinct discussion of ethical issues and best practices in clinical supervision.

Falender, C. A., & Shafranske, E. P. (2007). Competence in competency-based supervision practice: Construct and application. *Professional Psychology: Research and Practice, 38,* 232–240. http://dx.doi.org/10.1037/0735-7028.38.3.232

Defines competence as a construct and ethical requirement; discusses core competencies, metacompetence, and clinical competence; and offers recommendations to implement competency-based clinical supervision.

Falender, C. A., & Shafranske, E. P. (2012). The importance of competency-based clinical supervision and training in the twenty-first century: Why bother? *Journal of Contemporary Psychology, 42,* 129–137. http://dx.doi.org/10.1007/s10879-011-9198-9

Situates competency-based clinical supervision within the larger competencies movement, argues for a necessary shift in the culture of training and supervision, and identifies the "value-added" benefits of implementing the approach.

Falender, C. A., & Shafranske, E. P. (2014). Clinical supervision: The state of the art. *Journal of Clinical Psychology, 70,* 1030–1041. http://dx.doi.org/10.1002/jclp.22124

Highlights recent developments and best practices, including approaches to transform clinical supervision, and provides supervision vignette with verbatim excerpts and commentary.

Falender, C. A., Shafranske, E. P., & Olek, A. (2014). Competent clinical supervision: Emerging effective practices. *Counseling Psychology Quarterly, 27,* 393–408. http://dx.doi.org/10.1080/09515070.2014.934785

Summarizes best practices in competency-based clinical supervision, which can be used in implementation as well as for supervisor self-assessment.

Goodyear, R., Lichtenberg, J. W., Bang, K., & Gragg, J. B. (2014). Ten changes psychotherapists typically make as they mature into the role of supervisor. *Journal of Clinical Psychology, 70,* 1042–1050. http://dx.doi.org/10.1002/jclp.22125

Argues that supervisor development is best studied as dimensions and presents the results of study of 22 supervisors, including discussion of 10 themes and an illustrative case vignette.

Johnson, W. B., Barnett, J. E., Elman, N. S., Forrest, L., & Kaslow, N. J. (2012). The competent community: Toward a vital reformulation of professional ethics. *American Psychologist, 67,* 557–569. http://dx.doi.org/10.1037/a0027206

The authors propose a fundamental shift in the development of competence by including interdependent, collectivist, or communitarian perspectives.

Kaslow, N. J., Falender, C. A., & Grus, C. (2012). Valuing and practicing competency-based supervision: A transformational leadership perspective. *Training and Education in Professional Psychology, 6,* 47–54. http://dx.doi.org/10.1037/a0026704

A shift from a transactional to a transformational leadership style is required to facilitate the implementation of competency-based clinical supervision.

Soheilian, S. S., Inman, A. G., Klinger, R. S., Isenberg, D. S., & Kulp, L. E. (2014). Multicultural supervision: Supervisees' reflections on culturally competent supervision. *Counselling Psychology Quarterly, 27,* 379–392. http://dx.doi.org/10.1080/09515070.2014.961408

Reports the findings of a study of supervisees' perceived experiences of supervisor multicultural competence in supervision and its impact on supervisees' clinical work.

References

Abbass, A., Arthey, S., Elliott, J., Fedak, T., Nowoweiski, D., Markovski, J., & Nowoweiski, S. (2011). Web-conference supervision for advanced psychotherapy training: A practical guide. *Psychotherapy, 48*, 109–118. http://dx.doi.org/10.1037/a0022427

American Counseling Association. (2005). *ACA code of ethics*. Alexandria, VA: Author.

American Counseling Association. (2014). *2014 ACA code of ethics*. Alexandria, VA: Author.

American Psychological Association. (2010). *Ethical principles of psychologists and code of conduct (2002, Amended June 1, 2010)*. Retrieved from http://www.apa.org/ethics/code/index.aspx

American Psychological Association. (2013). *Guidelines for the practice of telepsychology*. Retrieved from http://www.apa.org/practice/guidelines/telepsychology.aspx

American Psychological Association. (2014). *Guidelines for clinical supervision in health service psychology*. Retrieved from http://www.apa.org/about/policy/guidelines-supervision.pdf

American Psychological Association. (2015). Guidelines for clinical supervision in health service psychology. *American Psychologist, 70*, 33–46. http://dx.doi.org/10.1037/a0038112

American Psychological Association. (Producer). (2016). *Competency-based supervision* [DVD]. Available from http://www.apa.org/pubs/videos/4310954.aspx

APA Presidential Task Force on Evidence-Based Practice. (2006). Evidence-based practice in psychology. *American Psychologist, 61*, 271–285. http://dx.doi.org/10.1037/0003-066X.61.4.271

Asay, P. A., & Lal, A. (2014). Who's Googled whom? Trainees' Internet and online social networking experiences, behaviors, and attitudes with clients and supervisors. *Training and Education in Professional Psychology, 8*(2), 105–111. http://dx.doi.org/10.1037/tep0000035

Association of State and Provincial Psychology Boards. (2003). *Final report of the ASPPB Task Force on Supervision Guidelines.* Montgomery, AL: Author.

Association of State and Provincial Psychology Boards. (2015). *Supervision guidelines for education and training leading to licensure as a health service provider.* Retrieved from http://c.ymcdn.com/sites/www.asppb.net/resource/resmgr/Guidelines/Final_Supervision_Guidelines.pdf

Balas, E. A., & Boren, S. A. (2000). Managing clinical knowledge for health care improvement. In J. van Bemmel & A. T. McCray (Eds.), *Yearbook of medical informatics* (pp. 65–70). Stuttgart, Germany: Schattauer.

Barnett, J. E. (2011). Utilizing technological innovations to enhance psychotherapy supervision, training, and outcomes. *Psychotherapy, 48,* 103–108. http://dx.doi.org/10.1037/a0023381

Barnett, J. E., & Molzon, C. H. (2014). Clinical supervision of psychotherapy: Essential ethics issues for supervisors and supervisees. *Journal of Clinical Psychology, 70*(11), 1051–1061. http://dx.doi.org/10.1002/jclp.22126

Bearman, S. K., Weisz, J. R., Chorpita, B. F., Hoagwood, K., Ward, A., Ugueto, A. M., . . . the Research Network on Youth Mental Health. (2013). More practice, less preach? The role of supervision processes and therapist characteristics in EBP implementation. *Administration and Policy in Mental Health, 40,* 518–529. http://dx.doi.org/10.1007/s10488-013-0485-5

Beauchamp, T. L., & Childress, J. F. (2009). *Principles of biomedical ethics* (6th ed.). New York, NY: Oxford University Press.

Beloit College. (2016). *2017 list.* Retrieved from https://www.beloit.edu/mindset/previouslists/2017/

Bernard, J. M., & Goodyear, R. K. (1998). *Fundamentals of clinical supervision* (2nd ed.). Needham Heights, MA: Allyn Bacon.

Bernard, J. M., & Goodyear, R. K. (2014). *Fundamentals of clinical supervision* (5th ed.). Boston, MA: Pearson.

Bieschke, K. J., & Mintz, L. B. (2012). Counseling psychology, model training values statement addressing diversity: History, current use, and future directions. *Training and Education in Professional Psychology, 6,* 196–203. http://dx.doi.org/10.1037/a0030810

Borders, L. D., Glosoff, H. L., Welfare, L. E., Hays, D. G., DeKruyf, L., Fernando, D. M., & Page, B. (2014). Best practices in clinical supervision: Evolution of a counseling specialty. *The Clinical Supervisor, 33*(1), 26–44. http://dx.doi.org/10.1080/07325223.2014.905225

Bordin, E. S. (1983). Supervision in counseling: II. Contemporary models of supervision: A working alliance based model of supervision. *The Counseling Psychologist, 11*, 35–42. http://dx.doi.org/10.1177/0011000083111007

Brown, L. S. (2016). *Supervision essentials for the feminist psychotherapy model of supervision.* Washington, DC: American Psychological Association. http://dx.doi.org/10.1037/14878-000

Brynolf, A., Johansson, S., Appelgren, E., Lynoe, N., & Edstedt Bonamy, A. K. (2013). Virtual colleagues, virtually colleagues—Physicians' use of Twitter: A population-based observational study. *BMJ Open, 3.* http://dx.doi.org/10.1136/bmjopen-2013-002988

Chow, D. L., Miller, S. D., Seidel, J. A., Kane, R. T., Thornton, J. A., & Andrews, W. P. (2015). The role of deliberate practice in the development of highly effective psychotherapists. *Psychotherapy, 52*, 337–345. http://dx.doi.org/10.1037/pst0000015

Clinton, B. K., Silverman, B. C., & Brendel, D. H. (2010). Patient-targeted Googling: The ethics of searching online for patient information. *Harvard Review of Psychiatry, 18*, 103–112. http://dx.doi.org/10.3109/10673221003683861

Crook-Lyon, R. E., Presnell, J., Silva, L., Suyama, M., & Stickney, J. (2011). Emergent supervisors: Comparing counseling center and non–counseling-center interns' supervisory training experiences. *Journal of College Counseling, 14*, 34–49. http://dx.doi.org/10.1002/j.2161-1882.2011.tb00062.x

Curry, J. F. (2015). Training implications of psychology's approach to conscience clause cases. *Training and Education in Professional Psychology, 9*(4), 275–278. http://dx.doi.org/10.1037/tep0000102

Davis, D. A., Mazmanian, P. E., Fordis, M., Harrison, R. V., Thorpe, K. E., & Perrier, L. (2006, September 6). Accuracy of physician self-assessment compared with observed measures of competence: A systematic review. *JAMA, 296*, 1094–1102. http://dx.doi.org/10.1001/jama.296.9.1094

Deane, F. P., Gonsalvez, C., Blackman, R., Saffioti, D., & Andresen, R. (2015). Issues in the development of e-supervision in professional psychology: A review. *Australian Psychologist, 50*, 241–247. http://dx.doi.org/10.1111/ap.12107

DeJong, S. M., Benjamin, S., Anzia, J. M., John, N., Boland, R. J., Lomax, J., & Rostain, A. L. (2012). Professionalism and the Internet in psychiatry: What to teach and how to teach it. *Academic Psychiatry, 36*, 356–362. http://dx.doi.org/10.1176/appi.ap.11050097

DeMers, S. T., & Schaffer, J. B. (2012). The regulation of professional psychology. In S. J. Knapp (Ed.), *APA handbook of ethics in psychology: Vol. 1. Moral foundations and common themes* (pp. 453–482). Washington, DC: American Psychological Association. http://dx.doi.org/10.1037/13271-018

Duan, C., & Roehlke, H. (2001). A descriptive "snapshot" of cross-racial supervision in university counseling center internships. *Journal of Multicultural Counseling and Development, 29,* 131–146. http://dx.doi.org/10.1002/j.2161-1912.2001. tb00510.x

Dunning, D., Heath, C., & Suls, J. M. (2004). Flawed self-assessment: Implications for health, education, and the workplace. *Psychological Science in the Public Interest, 5,* 69–106. http://dx.doi.org/10.1111/j.1529-1006.2004. 00018.x

Ellis, M. V., Berger, L., Hanus, A., Ayala, E. E., Swords, B. A., & Siembor, M. (2014). Inadequate and harmful clinical supervision: Testing a revised framework and assessing occurrence. *The Counseling Psychologist, 42,* 434–472. http://dx.doi.org/10.1177/0011000013508656

Elman, N. S., & Forrest, L. (2007). From trainee impairment to professional competence problems: Seeking new terminology that facilitates effective action. *Professional Psychology: Research and Practice, 38,* 501–509. http://dx.doi.org/ 10.1037/0735-7028.38.5.501

Epstein, R. M., & Hundert, E. M. (2002, January 9). Defining and assessing professional competence. *JAMA, 287,* 226–235. http://dx.doi.org/10.1001/ jama.287.2.226

Falender, C. A. (2014). Supervision outcomes: Beginning the journey beyond the emperor's new clothes. *Training and Education in Professional Psychology, 8,* 143–148. http://dx.doi.org/10.1037/tep0000066

Falender, C. A., Burnes, T., & Ellis, M. (2013). Introduction to major contribution: Multicultural clinical supervision and benchmarks: Empirical support informing practice and supervisor training. *The Counseling Psychologist, 41,* 8–27. http://dx.doi.org/10.1177/0011000012438417

Falender, C. A., Collins, C. J., & Shafranske, E. P. (2009). "Impairment" and performance issues in clinical supervision: After the 2008 ADA Amendments Act. *Training and Education in Professional Psychology,3,*240–249.http://dx.doi.org/ 10.1037/a0017153

Falender, C. A., Ellis, M. V., & Burnes, T. (2013). Response to reactions to major contribution: Multicultural clinical supervision and benchmarks. *The Counseling Psychologist, 41,*140–151. http://dx.doi.org/10.1177/0011000012464061

Falender, C. A., & Shafranske, E. P. (2004). *Clinical supervision: A competency-based approach.* Washington, DC: American Psychological Association. http:// dx.doi.org/10.1037/10806-000

Falender, C. A., & Shafranske, E. P. (2007). Competence in competency-based supervision practice: Construct and application. *Professional Psychology: Research and Practice, 38,*232–240. http://dx.doi.org/10.1037/0735-7028.38.3.232

Falender, C. A., & Shafranske, E. P. (Eds.). (2008). *Casebook for clinical supervision: A competency-based approach.* Washington, DC: American Psychological Association. http://dx.doi.org/10.1037/11792-000

Falender, C. A., & Shafranske, E. P. (2012a). *Getting the most out of clinical training and supervision: A guide for practicum students and interns.* Washington, DC: American Psychological Association. http://dx.doi.org/10.1037/13487-000

Falender, C. A., & Shafranske, E. P. (2012b). The importance of competency-based clinical supervision and training in the twenty-first century: Why bother? *Journal of Contemporary Psychotherapy, 42,* 129–137. http://dx.doi.org/10.1007/s10879-011-9198-9

Falender, C. A., & Shafranske, E. P. (2014). Clinical supervision in the era of competence. In W. B. Johnson & N. Kaslow (Eds.), *Oxford handbook of education and training in professional psychology* (pp. 291–313). New York, NY: Oxford Press.

Falender, C. A., Shafranske, E. P., & Falicov, C. (Eds.). (2014). *Multiculturalism and diversity in clinical supervision: A competency-based approach.* Washington, DC: American Psychological Association. http://dx.doi.org/10.1037/14370-000

Falender, C. A., Shafranske, E. P., & Ofek, A. (2014). Competent clinical supervision: Emerging effective practices. *Counselling Psychology Quarterly, 27,* 393–408. http://dx.doi.org/10.1080/09515070.2014.934785

Falicov, C. J. (2014). Psychotherapy and supervision as cultural encounters: The MECA framework. In C. A. Falender, E. P. Shafranske, & C. J. Falicov (Eds.), *Multiculturalism and diversity in clinical supervision: A competency-based approach* (pp. 29–58). Washington, DC: American Psychological Association. http://dx.doi.org/10.1037/14370-002

Farber, E. W., & Kaslow, N. J. (2010). Introduction to the special section: The role of supervision in ensuring the development of psychotherapy competencies across diverse theoretical perspectives. *Psychotherapy: Theory, Research, Practice, Training, 47,* 1–2. http://dx.doi.org/10.1037/a0018850

Farnan, J. M., Sulmasy, L. S., Worster, B. K., Chaudhry, H. J., Rhyne, J. A., & Arora, V. M. (2013). Online medical professionalism: Patient and public relationships: Policy statement from the American College of Physicians and the Federation of State Medical Boards. *Annals of Internal Medicine, 158,* 620–627. http://dx.doi.org/10.7326/0003-4819-158-8-201304160 00100

Foo Kune, N. M. R., & Rodolfa, E. R. (2013). Putting the benchmarks into practice: Multiculturally competent supervisors—effective supervision. *The Counseling Psychologist, 41,* 121–130. http://dx.doi.org/10.1177/0011000012453944

Forrest, L., Elman, N. S., Huprich, S. K., Veilleux, J. C., Jacobs, S. C., & Kaslow, N. J. (2013). Training direct ors' perceptions of faculty behaviors when dealing with trainee competence problems: A mixed method pilot study. *Training and Education in Professional Psychology, 7,* 23–32. http://dx.doi.org/10.1037/a0032068

Foster, V. A., & McAdams, C. R., III. (1999). The impact of client suicide in counselor training: Implications for counselor education and supervision. *Counselor Education and Supervision, 39,* 22–33. http://dx.doi.org/10.1002/j.1556-6978.1999.tb01787.x

Fouad, N. A., Grus, C. L., Hatcher, R. L., Kaslow, N. J., Hutchings, P. S., Madson, M. B., . . . Crossman, R. E. (2009). Competency benchmarks: A model for understanding and measuring competence in professional psychology across training levels. *Training and Education in Professional Psychology, 3*(4, Suppl.), S5–S26. http://dx.doi.org/10.1037/a0015832

Fox, S., & Duggan, M. (2013). *2012 health survey.* Retrieved from http://www.pewinternet.org/2013/01/15/methodology-7/

Gabbard, G. O., Kassaw, K. A., & Perez-Garcia, G. (2011). Professional boundaries in the era of the Internet. *Academic Psychiatry, 35,* 168–174. http://dx.doi.org/10.1176/appi.ap.35.3.168

Gelso, C. J., & Hayes, J. A. (2002). The management of countertransference. In J. C. Norcross (Ed.), *Psychotherapy relationships that work* (pp. 267–283). New York, NY: Oxford University Press.

Genuchi, M. C., Rings, J. A., Germek, M. D., & Cornish, J. A. E. (2015). Clinical supervisors' perceptions of the clarity and comprehensiveness of the supervision competencies framework. *Training and Education in Professional Psychology, 9*(1), 68–76. http://dx.doi.org/10.1037/tep0000064

George, D. R., & Green, M. J. (2012). Beyond good and evil: Exploring medical trainee use of social media. *Teaching and Learning in Medicine, 24,* 155–157. http://dx.doi.org/10.1080/10401334.2012.664972

Gonsalvez, C. J., & Calvert, F. L. (2014). Competency-based models of supervision: Principles and applications, promises and challenges. *Australian Psychologist, 49,* 200–208. http://dx.doi.org/10.1111/ap.12055

Goodyear, R., Lichtenberg, J. W., Bang, K., & Gragg, J. B. (2014). Ten changes psychotherapists typically make as they mature into the role of supervisor. *Journal of Clinical Psychology, 70,* 1042–1050. http://dx.doi.org/10.1002/jclp.22125

Gottlieb, M. C., Handelsman, M. M., & Knapp, S. (2008). Some principles for ethics education: Implementing the acculturation model. *Training and Education in Professional Psychology, 2,* 123–128. http://dx.doi.org/10.1037/1931-3918.2.3.123

Gottlieb, M. C., Robinson, K., & Younggren, J. N. (2007). Multiple relations in supervision: Guidance for administrators, supervisors, and students. *Professional Psychology: Research and Practice, 38,* 241–247. http://dx.doi.org/10.1037/0735-7028.38.3.241

Greysen, S. R., Kind, T., & Chretien, K. C. (2010). Online professionalism and the mirror of social media. *Journal of General Internal Medicine, 25,* 1227–1229. http://dx.doi.org/10.1007/s11606-010-1447-1

Grossl, A. B., Reese, R. J., Norsworthy, L. A., & Hopkins, N. B. (2014). Client feedback data in supervision: Effects on supervision and outcome. *Training and Education in Professional Psychology, 8,* 182–188. http://dx.doi.org/10.1037/tep0000025

Guy, J. D., Brown, C. K., & Poelstra, P. L. (1992). Safety concerns and protective measures used by psychotherapists. *Professional Psychology: Research and Practice, 23,* 421–423. http://dx.doi.org/10.1037/0735-7028.23.5.421

Hall-Marley, S. (2004). Therapist evaluation checklist. In C. A. Falender & E. P. Shafranske (Eds.), *Clinical supervision: A competency-based approach* (pp. 277–280). Washington, DC: American Psychological Association.

Hansen, N. D., Randazzo, K. V., Schwartz, A., Marshall, M., Kalis, D., Frazier, R., . . . Norvig, G. (2006). Do we practice what we preach? An exploratory survey of multicultural psychotherapy competencies. *Professional Psychology: Research and Practice, 37,* 66–74. http://dx.doi.org/10.1037/0735-7028.37.1.66

Hatcher, R. L., Fouad, N. A., Grus, C. L., Campbell, L. F., McCutcheon, S. R., & Leahy, K. L. (2013). Competency benchmarks: Practical steps toward a culture of competence. *Training and Education in Professional Psychology, 7,* 84–91. http://dx.doi.org/10.1037/a0029401

Hayes, J. A., & Gelso, C. J. (2001). Clinical implications of research on countertransference: Science informing practice. *Journal of Clinical Psychology, 57,* 1041–1051. http://dx.doi.org/10.1002/jclp.1072

Inman, A. G., Hutman, H., Pendse, A., Devdas, L., Luu, L., & Ellis, M. V. (2014). Current trends concerning supervisors, supervisees, and clients in clinical supervision. In C. E. Watkins & D. L. Milne (Eds.), *The Wiley international handbook of clinical supervision* (pp. 61–102). Malden, MA: Wiley. http://dx.doi.org/10.1002/9781118846360.ch4

International Union of Psychological Science. (2008). *Universal declaration of ethical principles for psychologists.* Retrieved from http://www.iupsys.net/about/governance/universal-declaration-of-ethical-principles-for-psychologists.html

Jacobs, S. C., Huprich, S. K., Grus, C. L., Cage, E. A., Elman, N. S., Forrest, L., . . . Kaslow, N. J. (2011). Trainees with professional competencies problems: Preparing trainers for difficult but necessary conversations. *Training and Education in Professional Psychology, 5,* 175–184. http://dx.doi.org/10.1037/a0024656

Jain, A., Petty, E. M., Jaber, R. M., Tackett, S., Purkiss, J., Fitzgerald, J., & White, C. (2014). What is appropriate to post on social media? Ratings from students, faculty members and the public. *Medical Education, 48,* 157–169. http://dx.doi.org/10.1111/medu.12282

Jain, S. H. (2009). Practicing medicine in the age of Facebook. *The New England Journal of Medicine, 361,* 649–651. http://dx.doi.org/10.1056/NEJMp0901277

Jernigan, M. M., Green, C. E., Helms, J. E., Perez-Gualdron, L., & Henze, K. (2010). An examination of people of color supervision dyads: Racial identity matters as much as race. *Training and Education in Professional Psychology, 4,* 62–73. http://dx.doi.org/10.1037/a0018110

Johnson, W. B., Barnett, J. E., Elman, N. S., Forrest, L., & Kaslow, N. J. (2013). The competence constellation model: A communitarian approach to support professional competence. *Professional Psychology: Research and Practice, 44,* 343–354. http://dx.doi.org/10.1037/a0033131

Johnson, W. B., Barnett, J. E., Elman, N. S., Forrest, L., Schwartz-Mette, R., & Kaslow, N. J. (2014). Preparing trainees for lifelong competence: Creating a communitarian training culture. *Training and Education in Professional Psychology, 8,* 211–220. http://dx.doi.org/10.1037/tep0000048

Johnson, W. B., Elman, N. S., Forrest, L., Robiner, W. N., Rodolfa, E., & Schaffer, J. B. (2008). Addressing professional competence problems in trainees: Some ethical considerations. *Professional Psychology: Research and Practice, 39,* 589–599. http://dx.doi.org/10.1037/a0014264

Julea Ward v. Polite, No. 10-2100/2145 (E. D. Michigan, 2012).

Kaduvettoor, A., O'Shaughnessy, T., Mori, Y., Beverly, C., Weatherford, R. D., & Ladany, N. (2009). Helpful and hindering multicultural events in group supervision: Climate and multicultural competence. *The Counseling Psychologist, 37,* 786–820. http://dx.doi.org/10.1177/0011000009333984

Kagan, H., & Kagan, N. I. (1997). Interpersonal process recall: Influencing human interaction. In C. E. Watkins, Jr. (Ed.), *Handbook of psychotherapy supervision* (pp. 296–309). New York, NY: Wiley.

Kaslow, N. J. (2004). Competencies in professional psychology. *American Psychologist, 59,* 774–781. http://dx.doi.org/10.1037/0003-066X.59.8.774

Kaslow, N. J., & Bell, K. D. (2008). A competency-based approach to supervision. In C. A. Falender & E. P. Shafranske (Eds.), *Casebook for clinical supervision: A competency-based approach* (pp. 17–38). Washington, DC: American Psychological Association. http://dx.doi.org/10.1037/11792-002

Kaslow, N. J., Falender, C. A., & Grus, C. (2012). Valuing and practicing competency-based supervision: A transformational leadership perspective. *Training and Education in Professional Psychology, 6,* 47–54. http://dx.doi.org/10.1037/a0026704

Keeton v. Anderson-Wiley, 664 F. 3d 865 (2011).

Kiesler, D. J. (2001). Therapist countertransference: In search of common themes and empirical referents. *Journal of Clinical Psychology, 57,* 1053–1063. http://dx.doi.org/10.1002/jclp.1073

Kleespies, P. M. (1993). The stress of patient suicidal behavior: Implications for interns and training programs in psychology. *Professional Psychology: Research and Practice, 24,* 477–482. http://dx.doi.org/10.1037/0735-7028. 24.4.477

Kleespies, P. M., & Dettmer, E. L. (2000). The stress of patient emergencies for the clinician: Incidence, impact, and means of coping. *Journal of Clinical Psychology, 56,* 1353–1369. http://dx.doi.org/10.1002/1097-4679(200010)56:10<1353:: AID-JCLP7>3.0.CO;2-3

Knapp, S. J., Gottlieb, M. C., & Handelsman, M. M. (2015). *Ethical dilemmas in psychotherapy: Positive approaches to decision making.* Washington, DC: American Psychological Association.

Knapp, S. J., & VandeCreek, L. D. (2006). *Practical ethics for psychologists: A positive approach.* Washington, DC: American Psychological Association. http://dx.doi.org/10.1037/11331-000

Knox, S., Burkard, A. W., Jackson, J. A., Schaack, A. M., & Hess, S. A. (2006). Therapists-in-training who experience a client suicide: Implications for supervision. *Professional Psychology: Research and Practice, 37,* 547–557. http://dx.doi.org/10.1037/0735-7028.37.5.547

Kolb, D. A. (1984). *Experiential learning: Experience as the source of learning and development.* Englewood Cliffs, NJ: Prentice Hall.

Koocher, G. P., & Keith-Spiegel, P. (2008). *Ethics in psychology and the mental health professions: Standards and cases* (3rd ed.). New York, NY: Oxford University Press.

Kotter, J. (1996). *Leading change.* Boston, MA: Harvard Business School Press.

Ladany, N. (2014). The ingredients of supervisor failure. *Journal of Clinical Psychology, 70,* 1094–1103. http://dx.doi.org/10.1002/jclp.22130

Ladany, N., Lehrman-Waterman, D., Molinaro, M., & Wolgast, B. (1999). Psychotherapy supervisor ethical practices: Adherence to guidelines, the supervisory working alliance, and supervisee satisfaction. *The Counseling Psychologist, 27,* 443–475. http://dx.doi.org/10.1177/0011000099273008

Ladany, N., Mori, Y., & Mehr, K. W. (2013). Effective and ineffective supervision. *The Counseling Psychologist, 41,* 28–47. http://dx.doi.org/10.1177/0011000012442648

Lamb, D. H., Presser, N. R., Ptost, K. S., Baum, M. C., Jackson, V. R., & Jarvis, P. (1987). Confronting professional impairment during the internship: Identification, due process, and remediation. *Professional Psychology: Research and Practice, 18,* 597–603. http://dx.doi.org/10.1037/0735-7028.18.6.597

Logie, C., Bogo, M., Regehr, C., & Regehr, G. (2013). A critical appraisal of the use of standardized client simulations in social work education. *Journal of Social Work Education, 49,* 66–80.

Magnuson, S., Wilcoxon, S. A., & Norem, K. (2000). A profile of lousy supervision: Experienced counselors' perspectives. *Counselor Education and Supervision, 39*, 189–202. http://dx.doi.org/10.1002/j.1556-6978.2000.tb01231.x

Meichenbaum, D. (2007). Stress inoculation training: A preventative and treatment approach. In R. Lehrer, R. Woolfolk, & W. Sime (Eds.), *Principles and practice of stress management* (3rd ed., pp. 497–518). New York, NY: Guilford Press.

Milne, D. (2008). Trainee competence Checklist (TraCC). In C. A. Falender & E. P. Shafranske (Eds.), *Casebook for clinical supervision: A competency-based approach.* (pp. 235–243). Washington, DC: American Psychological Association.

Milne, D. (2009). *Evidence-based clinical supervision: Principles and practice.* Leicester, England: Malden Blackwell.

Milne, D. L. (2014). Toward an evidence-based approach to clinical supervision. In C. E. Watkins & D. L. Milne (Eds.), *The Wiley international handbook of clinical supervision* (pp. 38–60). Malden, MA: Wiley. http://dx.doi.org/10.1002/9781118846360.ch3

Norcross, J. C., & Guy, J. D. (2005). Therapist self-care checklist. In G. P. Koocher, J. C. Norcross, & S. S. Hill, III (Eds.), *Psychologists' desk reference* (2nd ed., pp. 677–682). New York, NY: Oxford University Press.

Norcross, J. C., & Lambert, M. J. (2014). Relationship science and practice in psychotherapy: Closing commentary. *Psychotherapy, 51*, 398–403. http://dx.doi.org/10.1037/a0037418

Osman, A., Wardle, A., & Caesar, R. (2012). Online professionalism and Facebook—Falling through the generation gap. *Medical Teacher, 34*, e549–e556. http://dx.doi.org/10.3109/0142159X.2012.668624

Pabian, Y. L., Welfel, E., & Beebe, R. S. (2009). Psychologists' knowledge of their states' laws pertaining to Tarasoff-type situations. *Professional Psychology: Research and Practice, 40*, 8–14. http://dx.doi.org/10.1037/a0014784

Pakdaman, S., Shafranske, E. P., & Falender, C. (2015). Ethics in supervision: Consideration of the supervisory alliance and countertransference management of psychology doctoral students. *Ethics & Behavior, 25*, 427–441. http://dx.doi.org/10.1080/10508422.2014.947415

Pettifor, J., Sinclair, C., & Falender, C. A. (2014). Ethical supervision: Harmonizing rules and ideals in a globalizing world. *Training and Education in Professional Psychology, 8*(2), 1–10.

Ponce, B. A., Determann, J. R., Boohaker, H. A., Sheppard, E., McGwin, G., Jr., & Theiss, S. (2013). Social networking profiles and professionalism issues in residency applicants: An original study-cohort study. *Journal of Surgical Education, 70*, 502–507. http://dx.doi.org/10.1016/j.jsurg.2013.02.005

Pope, K. S. (1994). *Sexual involvement with therapists: Patient assessment, subsequent therapy, forensics.* Washington, DC: American Psychological Association. http://dx.doi.org/10.1037/10154-000

Pope, K. S., Sonne, J. L., & Greene, B. (2006). *What therapists don't talk about and why: Understanding taboos that hurt us and our clients.* Washington, DC: American Psychological Association. http://dx.doi.org/10.1037/11413-000

Pope, K. S., & Tabachnick, B. G. (1993). Therapists' anger, hate, fear, and sexual feelings: National survey of therapists' responses, client characteristics, critical events, formal complaints, and training. *Professional Psychology: Research and Practice, 24,* 142–152. http://dx.doi.org/10.1037/0735-7028.24.2.142

Porter, N., & Vasquez, M. (1997). Covision: Feminist supervision, process, and collaboration. In J. Worell & N. Johnson (Eds.), *Shaping the future of feminist psychology: Education, research, and practice* (pp. 155–171). Washington, DC: American Psychological Association. http://dx.doi.org/10.1037/10245-007

Reese, R. J., Aldarondo, F., Anderson, C. R., Lee, S. J., Miller, T. W., & Burton, D. (2009). Telehealth in clinical supervision: A comparison of supervision formats. *Journal of Telemedicine and Telecare, 15,* 356–361. http://dx.doi.org/10.1258/jtt.2009.090401

Rings, J. A., Genuchi, M. C., Hall, M. D., Angelo, M., & Cornish, J. A. E. (2009). Is there consensus among predoctoral internship training directors regarding clinical supervision competencies? A descriptive analysis. *Training and Education in Professional Psychology, 3*(3), 140–147. http://dx.doi.org/10.1037/a0015054

Roberts, M. C., Borden, K. A., Christiansen, M. D., & Lopez, S. J. (2005). Fostering a culture shift: Assessment of competence in the education and careers of professional psychologists. *Professional Psychology: Research and Practice, 36,* 355–361. http://dx.doi.org/10.1037/0735-7028.36.4.355

Rodolfa, E., Bent, R., Eisman, E., Nelson, P., Rehm, L., & Ritchie, P. (2005). A cube model for competency development: Implications for psychology educators and regulators. *Professional Psychology: Research and Practice, 36,* 347–354. http://dx.doi.org/10.1037/0735-7028.36.4.347

Rousmaniere, T., Abbass, A., & Frederickson, J. (2014). New developments in technology-assisted supervision and training: A practical overview. *Journal of Clinical Psychology, 70,* 1082–1093. http://dx.doi.org/10.1002/jclp.22129

Safran, J. D., Muran, J. C., Stevens, C., & Rothman, M. (2008). A relational approach to supervision: Addressing ruptures in the alliance. In C. A. Falender & E. P. Shafranske (Eds.), *Casebook for clinical supervision: A competency-based approach* (pp. 137–157). Washington, DC: American Psychological Association. http://dx.doi.org/10.1037/11792-007

Sarnat, J. E. (2016). *Supervision essentials for psychodynamic psychotherapies.* Washington, DC: American Psychological Association. http://dx.doi.org/10.1037/14802-000

Schulman, C. I., Kuchkarian, F. M., Withum, K. F., Boecker, F. S., & Graygo, J. M. (2013). Influence of social networking websites on medical school and residency selection process. *Postgraduate Medical Journal, 89,* 126–130. http://dx.doi.org/10.1136/postgradmedj-2012-131283

Sehgal, R., Saules, K., Young, A., Grey, M. J., Gillem, A. R., Nabors, N. A., . . . Jefferson, S. (2011). Practicing what we know: Multicultural counseling competence among clinical psychology trainees and experienced multicultural psychologists. *Cultural Diversity and Ethnic Minority Psychology, 17,* 1–10. http://dx.doi.org/10.1037/a0021667

Shafranske, E. P. (Ed.). (1996). *Religion and the clinical practice of psychology.* Washington, DC: American Psychological Association.

Shafranske, E. P. (2013). Addressing religiousness and spirituality in psychotherapy: Advancing evidence-based practice. In R. F. Paloutzian & C. L. Park (Eds.), *Handbook of the psychology of religion and spirituality* (2nd ed., pp. 596–616). New York, NY: Guilford.

Shafranske, E. P. (2014). Addressing religiousness and spirituality as clinically relevant cultural features in supervision. In C. A. Falender, E. P. Shafranske, & C. J. Falicov (Eds.), *Multiculturalism and diversity in clinical supervision: A competency-based approach* (pp. 181–207). Washington, DC: American Psychological Association. http://dx.doi.org/10.1037/14370-008

Shafranske, E. P., & Cummings, J. P. (2013). Religious and spiritual beliefs, affiliations, and practices of psychologists. In K. I. Pargament (Ed.), *APA handbook of psychology, religion, and spirituality: Vol. 2. An applied psychology of religion and spirituality* (pp. 23–41). Washington, DC: American Psychological Association. http://dx.doi.org/10.1037/14046-002

Shafranske, E. P., & Falender, C. A. (2008). Supervision addressing personal factors and countertransference. In C. A. Falender & E. P. Shafranske (Eds.), *Casebook for clinical supervision: A competency-based approach* (pp. 97–120). Washington, DC: American Psychological Association. http://dx.doi.org/10.1037/11792-005

Shafranske, E. P., & Falender, C. A. (2016). Clinical supervision. In J. C. Norcross, G. R. VandenBos, & D. K. Freedheim (Eds.), *APA handbook of clinical psychology: Vol. 5. Education and profession* (pp. 175–196). Washington, DC: American Psychological Association.

Singh, A., & Chun, K. Y. S. (2010). "From the margins to the center": Moving towards a resilience-based model of supervision for queer people of color supervisors. *Training and Education in Professional Psychology, 4,* 36–46. http://dx.doi.org/10.1037/a0017373

Sobell, L. C., Manor, H. L., Sobell, M. B., & Dum, M. (2008). Self-critiques of audio-taped therapy sessions: A motivational procedure for facilitating feedback during supervision. *Training and Education in Professional Psychology, 2,* 151–155. http://dx.doi.org/10.1037/1931-3918.2.3.151

Soheilian, S. S., Inman, A. G., Klinger, R. S., Isenberg, D. S., & Kulp, L. E. (2014). Multicultural supervision: Supervisees' reflections on culturally competent supervision. *Counselling Psychology Quarterly, 27,* 379–392. http://dx.doi.org/10.1080/09515070.2014.961408

Spiegelman, J. S., Jr., & Werth, J. L., Jr. (2004). Don't forget about me. *Women & Therapy, 28,* 35–57. http://dx.doi.org/10.1300/J015v28n01_04

Sterkenburg, A., Barach, P., Kalkman, C., Gielen, M., & ten Cate, O. (2010). When do supervising physicians decide to entrust residents with unsupervised tasks? *Academic Medicine, 85,* 1408–1417. http://dx.doi.org/10.1097/ACM.0b013e3181eab0ec

Stinson, J. (2014). *Password protected: States pass anti-snooping laws.* Retrieved from http://www.pewtrusts.org/en/research-and-analysis/blogs/stateline/2014/07/08/password-protected-states-pass-anti-snooping-laws

Sue, D. W., Capodilupo, C. M., Torino, G. C., Bucceri, J. M., Holder, A. M. B., Nadal, K. L., & Esquilin, M. (2007). Racial microaggressions in everyday life: Implications for clinical practice. *American Psychologist, 62,* 271–286. http://dx.doi.org/10.1037/0003-066X.62.4.271

Thomas, J. T. (2010). *The ethics of supervision and consultation: Practical guidance for mental health professionals.* Washington, DC: American Psychological Association. http://dx.doi.org/10.1037/12078-000

Tsong, Y., & Goodyear, R. K. (2014). Assessing supervision's clinical and multicultural impacts: The Supervision Outcome Scale's psychometric properties. *Training and Education in Professional Psychology, 8,* 189–195. http://dx.doi.org/10.1037/tep0000049

Varela, J. G., & Conroy, M. A. (2012). Professional competencies in forensic psychology. *Professional Psychology: Research and Practice, 43,* 410–421. http://dx.doi.org/10.1037/a0026776

Vargas, L. A., Porter, N., & Falender, C. A. (2008). Supervision, culture, and context. In C. A. Falender & E. P. Shafranske (Eds.), *Casebook for clinical supervision: A competency-based approach* (pp. 121–136). Washington, DC: American Psychological Association. http://dx.doi.org/10.1037/11792-006

Vasquez, M. (2014). Foreword. In C. F. Falender, E. P. Shafranske, & C. Falicov (Eds.), *Multiculturalism and diversity in clinical supervision: A competency-based approach* (pp. xi–xv). Washington, DC: American Psychological Association.

Vespia, K. M., Heckman-Stone, C., & Delworth, U. (2002). Describing and facilitating effective supervision behavior in counseling trainees. *Psychotherapy:*

Theory, Research, Practice, Training, 39, 56–65. http://dx.doi.org/10.1037/0033-3204.39.1.56

Wall, A. (2009). *Psychology interns' perceptions of supervisor ethical behavior* (Doctoral dissertation). Available from ProQuest Dissertations and Theses database. (AAT 3359934)

Ward v. Wilbanks, No. 09-CV-112 37, 2010 U.S. Dist. WL 3026428 (E. D. Michigan, July 26, 2010).

Watkins, C. E., Jr. (2014). The supervisory alliance as quintessential integrative variable. *Journal of Contemporary Psychotherapy, 44,* 151–161. http://dx.doi.org/10.1007/s10879-013-9252-x

Watkins, C. E., & Milne, D. L. (Eds.). (2014). *The Wiley international handbook of clinical supervision.* Malden, MA: Wiley. http://dx.doi.org/10.1002/9781118846360

Wester, S. R., Danforth, L., & Olle, C. (2013). Social networking sites and the evaluation of applicants and students in applied training programs in psychology. *Training and Education in Professional Psychology, 7,* 145–154. http://dx.doi.org/10.1037/a0032376

Williams, E. F., Dunning, D., & Kruger, J. (2013). The hobgoblin of consistency: Algorithmic judgment strategies underlie inflated self-assessments of performance. *Journal of Personality and Social Psychology, 104,* 976–994. http://dx.doi.org/10.1037/a0032416

Winnicott, D. (1986). The theory of the parent–infant relationship. In P. Buckley (Ed.), *Essential papers on object relations* (pp. 233–253). New York, NY: New York University Press.

Worthen, V. E., & Lambert, M. J. (2007). Outcome oriented supervision: Advantages of adding systematic client tracking to supportive consultations. *Counselling & Psychotherapy Research, 7,* 48–53. http://dx.doi.org/10.1080/14733140601140873

Zur, O., Williams, M. H., Lehavot, K., & Knapp, S. (2009). Psychotherapist self-disclosure and transparency in the Internet age. *Professional Psychology, Research and Practice, 40,* 22–30. http://dx.doi.org/10.1037/a0014745

Index

About the Authors

Carol A. Falender, PhD, is coauthor of *Clinical Supervision: A Competency-Based Approach* and *Getting the Most Out of Clinical Training and Supervision: A Guide for Practicum Students and Interns* with Edward P. Shafranske, coeditor of *Casebook for Clinical Supervision: A Competency-Based Approach* with Edward P. Shafranske, and coeditor of *Multiculturalism and Diversity in Clinical Supervision: A Competency-Based Approach* with Edward P. Shafranske and Celia J. Falicov. She was a member of the Supervision Guidelines Group of the Association of State and Provincial Psychology Boards and chair of the Supervision Guidelines Task Force of the Board of Educational Affairs of the American Psychological Association (APA). She directed APA-approved internship programs at child and family guidance clinics for over 20 years. Dr. Falender is a fellow of APA and was president of APA Division 37, Society for Child and Family Policy and Practice. She is an adjunct professor at Pepperdine University, clinical professor in the UCLA Department of Psychology, co-chair of the Los Angeles County Psychological Association Ethics Committee, and chair of the California Psychological Association Continuing Education Committee.

Edward P. Shafranske, PhD, ABPP, is a professor of psychology, Muriel Lipsey Chair in Clinical and Counseling Psychology, and director of the PsyD program in clinical psychology at Pepperdine University. In addition, he serves as associate clinical professor of psychiatry (voluntary), School of Medicine, University of California, Irvine, and maintains a clinical practice in Irvine, California. He has published widely in the field of clinical supervision. His books include *Clinical Supervision: A Competency-Based Approach* (with Carol A. Falender); *Getting the Most Out of Clinical Training and Supervision: A Guide for Practicum Students and Interns* (with Carol A. Falender); *Casebook for Clinical Supervision: A Competency-Based Approach* (with Carol A. Falender) and *Multiculturalism and Diversity in Clinical Supervision: A Competency-Based Approach* (with Carol A. Falender and Celia J. Falicov). Dr. Shafranske is a fellow of APA (Divisions 12, 29, 36), served twice as president of APA Division 36, and has been recognized for his contributions to the field of psychology by the California Psychological Association. Having supervised graduate students, postdoctoral clinicians, and psychiatric residents, he strives to make theory and research accessible to the everyday practice of clinical supervision.